GROWING UP WITH POETRY

GROWING UP WITH POETRY

an anthology for secondary schools

edited by David Rubadiri

Heinemann International
a division of Heinemann Educational Books Ltd
Halley Court, Jordan Hill, Oxford OX2 8EJ

Heinemann Educational Boleswa
PO Box 10103, Village Post Office, Gaborone, Botswana

OXFORD   LONDON   EDINBURGH
MELBOURNE   SYDNEY   AUCKLAND
IBADAN   NAIROBI   GABORONE
KINGSTON   PORTSMOUTH NH (USA)
SINGAPORE   MADRID

ISBN 0–435–92007–3
© Selection of poems David Rubadiri 1989
© Questions Liz Gerschel 1989
First published 1989

Illustrated by Matilda Harrison

British Library Cataloguing in Publication Data

Growing up with poetry: an anthology for secondary schools. (African
writers series. Heinemann African poets)
1. Poetry in English. African writers to 1945. Anthologies. For African
students. For schools
I. Rubadiri, David
821

Set in Meridien by Wilmaset, Birkenhead, Wirral
Printed and bound by Butler and Tanner Ltd., Frome and London

CONTENTS

VILLAGE LIFE

SEPARATION

POWER

FREEDOM

Before reading questions **70**

QUESTIONS

GLOSSARY   111

ACKNOWLEDGEMENTS   112

FOREWORD

The title of this anthology 'Growing up with Poetry' comes to you as a plea. A prayer to parents and teachers who have made the study and love of poetry too much of a *getting on* 'chore' to our youth. A people without a 'song' will carry dying souls. The pain of listening to youth living on the noises of foreign 'pop verses' is a cry of admonition to those who have ceased to care for values, as human beings in independent Africa today. They have lost interest in singing songs of praise to God. They are now even more tired of singing songs of praise to mere mortals on roadside parades. Is Africa to become a soulless, songless nation?

This anthology for Secondary Schools is an invitation to the young to rediscover their national heritage begun in the oral tradition. A poem a day soothes, heals, mends, teaches and inspires the family of Man, bird, beast and flower.

> *Modimo, tshegofatsa Africa . . .*   God, bless Africa
> *Lebelela bana ba gagwe*   Guard her children
> *Mme o e neye kagiso*   and give her peace.
>
> (Setswana)

DEDICATION

To all my students and colleagues at Makerere University, Nairobi University, University of Ife, Northwestern University USA, University of Botswana and dear Soche Hill College, Malawi. Your love for poetry made us friends for a lifetime.

To my family, the clan Rubadiri, whose patience and love is always beyond comprehension.

To my old school, Kings College, Budo, Uganda and the two headmasters, Lord Hemmingford and Timothy Cobb, who made me understand the beauty and growth of life in literature.

DAVID RUBADIRI

INTRODUCTION

To the Student

Have you ever thought that poems are very like people? Before you read any of the poems in this book, think about some of the people you know, especially your friends. How did you feel about them when you first met them? Sometimes you like someone immediately; other people take longer to get to know — maybe you don't even like them much at first. Then, gradually, as you get to know them, you begin to appreciate qualities in them which you couldn't see when you first met. Sometimes our best friends come from friendships which grow slowly.

Poetry is a bit like that. It is about the way we feel. Sometimes a poem is immediately enjoyable: it makes you smile or laugh out loud. Sometimes it reminds you of something you have experienced; you think 'How true — that's exactly what I feel, but I didn't think of putting it like that.' At other times a poem may be hard to understand at the first or even the second reading, but when you have become more familiar with it, you can begin to understand what the poet is really saying.

Occasionally, poems like that become your favourites. So you see, poems are like people you meet.

What makes poetry different from other literature? The poet is using the same language, and describing the same world, so what is the difference?

First of all, most poems are short, compared to a short story or a novel. But don't confuse length and density. A poet has to convey her or his ideas in fewer words and lines. This means that even a very short poem can contain very profound and complex ideas: there is an example of this in Grace Nichols' poem, *Epilogue* (page 50). It also means that poets make all their words really work for them; most poets draft and redraft their work until they are satisfied that the poem says exactly what they want it to. When you write, you too experiment with ideas and redraft your work until you're satisfied; this is a sensible way of becoming a better writer.

The second point about poetry is the way that it sounds when it is spoken aloud. All poems have a rhythm which is deliberately intended to create a pattern of sound. Sometimes the rhythm is strong and obvious; sometimes it is regular so that you could beat a drum to it. This is especially true of oral poems which are intended to be sung, chanted or recited. Sometimes the rhythm is less obvious, but it is still there. When we read poetry in books, we can see how the patterns are formed by the way the poem is printed in lines on the page, but we sometimes forget that poems are made to be said aloud. Try reading the poems in this book aloud to yourself and you will hear the rhythms and patterns of sound for yourself.

Of course, some poems have rhyme as well as rhythm, but not all. Rhyme is satisfying to hear and it is easy to remember: it can make poems sound musical. For these reasons, poems which are part of oral literature (traditional poems, children's poems and popular songs, for example) often rhyme. Whether poems rhyme or not, the sound patterns made by the rhythm and the words are very important.

The third point is the most important of all. Poets use language in a unique way. They don't just shape it into patterns of sound and rhythm, they use it in entirely new ways, in order to take the reader by surprise – make her or him sit up and look at something in a new light that has been taken for granted. Poets do this, often using quite simple words, by putting ideas together in a new way. Sometimes they make comparisons between things or use contrasts that startle us, to create images which will lead to deeper understanding. For example, Bonus Zimunya's poem, *Old Granny*, (page 40) starts like this:

A little freezing spider

Legs and arms gathered in her chest

The poet is using the image of the spider with its legs and arms drawn in to describe the old woman. He is relying on his readers to transfer what they know about the way spiders sit to the old woman, so that they can picture her more clearly in their minds and understand something about her circumstances. The image of the spider doesn't just suggest how she looks but what has made her look like that. You will be introduced, in this anthology, to the different kinds of expression and unique language used in poetry. There is a list of these special terms at the back of the book.

Reading poetry is not a passive exercise, you see: the reader has to be involved in it — like making friends with someone new. A poem which works well always says more than it seems to say when you first read it. That's why it is important to read a poem several times, to give you a chance to think about it, to share it with others, to explore the way the poet uses the language, the meanings and the sounds. But when you are reading a poem for the first time, remember that it is not necessary to understand every word in order to understand what the poet is trying to say.

Remember that enjoying poetry is not just reading the poems in one anthology. Poetry is a creative process: each poem has been carefully shaped and reshaped. You can be part of this process too. Try writing your own poems, about your family, your home, your feelings about anything that is important to you. Experiment with language — try different patterns of your poems and create your own images. If they don't work, try them again in another way. Collect poems that you like (in different languages) and make your own anthology.

Above all, enjoy, poetry. As Eve Merriam says in *How to eat a poem*:

> Don't be polite.
> Bite in.
> Pick it up with your fingers and lick the juice that may run
> down your chin.
> It is ready and ripe now, whenever you are.

Note: All poems accompanied by the symbol ◆ appear in *A closer look* sections.

To the Teacher

Many young people say they don't like poetry. This may have
something to do with the way they are introduced to poetry in the
classroom. As children we all enjoy songs, rhymes and riddles. As
students progress through junior and senior secondary school, they
are taught poetry which is more formal and more challenging.
Somewhere along the line their enjoyment of poetry often gets lost.

Why read poetry?

Reading for pleasure and understanding

Poetry is a pleasure to hear and to read; a well-made poem is
intensely satisfying to listen to in its rhythms and the patterns of
words and images it creates, in the same sort of way that visual art
is satisfying to see. Similarly, there are an infinite number of poems
that can please us, according to our needs, understandings and the
mood we are in. Poetry helps us to express our feelings and it helps
us to understand the feelings of others. Sometimes it helps us to
resolve the paradoxes of life; it explores human dilemmas and
preserves cultures and traditions as well as forging new dynamic
growth. As Okot p'Bitek said in a lecture published after his death
in *Artist, the ruler* (Heinemann Kenya, 1986), poets are among

> 'the few men and women, the supreme artists, the imaginative
> creators of their time, who form the consciousness of their
> time. They respond deeply and intuitively to what is
> happening, what has happened and what will happen.'

But poetry is not only the domain of the few: all of us have it in
us to be poets. What students also lose when they lose their
pleasure in poetry, is the confidence to try writing poetry
themselves. Another reason for reading poetry then, is to preserve
the poet in all of us.

Reading for study

Finally, there is the pressure of exams. Examining bodies, quite
rightly, regard poetry as an essential part of the study of literature.
The danger is, though, that in studying poetry for exam purposes,
the pleasure of it is lost in a welter of technical detail.

It may be that teachers will have deliberately to separate these two approaches, (reading for pleasure and reading for study) at least in their own minds. They can then ensure that they create opportunities for all their students to enjoy poetry for its own sake, while at other times concentrating on exploring the language and structures of poems.

One of the problems for students is that the study of poetry is often neglected at junior secondary level. Then, when they reach the upper forms, they find themselves thrown in at the deep end and, with almost no preparation, are expected to analyse and interpret poems which might be quite complex in language, structure and theme. As they progress through school, students should be able to grow with their poetry. The poetry of childhood need not be seen as separate from the poetry we study in school. In defining the aims of the poetry component of your English and Literature in English courses, you will need to consider what students should learn about poetry in junior and intermediate forms and how this can most effectively be achieved.

First and foremost, students should enjoy poetry. The poems in this anthology offer enjoyment on different levels: some will have an immediate impact on your students, while others will demand more reading and reflection. Encourage students to engage with both the accessible and the more challenging poems and to enjoy both.

The language of poetry
What's it all about?

Students should be acquiring the ability to understand and interpret the unique language of poetry. What makes the language of poetry unique is addressed in more detail in the notes to the student. Sometimes the ways that language is used in poetry can be difficult for those who speak English as a first language; often for those learning English as a second language it can create even more barriers.

Students will quickly lose interest when faced with a poem whose structure is complex and vocabulary obscure. Reading poems aloud helps here: students can begin to enjoy the sounds and rhythms of the poem and its richness of language. The most important point is that it is not necessary to understand every word in a poem in order to understand what it is trying to tell us. It is often a good idea to let students form a first impression of a poem's meaning and richness and come back to it later for a more intensive exploration. Certainly it may take students longer to understand the more complex language of English poets of earlier times, such as Donne and Shakespeare, but with careful preparation (and the questions suggested in this anthology are there to provide a helpful framework), poems such as *Let me not to the marriage of true minds* (page 7) and *Death, be not proud* (page 31) can be enjoyed by students of all abilities.

Making comparisons

An important part of understanding the language of poetry is learning about the importance of 'making comparisons: seeing how one thing is like another and in a new way' (George Macbeth, *Poetry for today*, Longman, 1984). Poets use comparison a great deal and for a variety of purposes: it enables them to convey shades of meaning in just a few words and to open up a whole, new, imaginative world to the reader. The mind pictures that students create from images that compare an old woman to a spider (*Old Granny*, page 40) or a bull to a raincloud (*The magnificent bull*, page 37) will greatly enhance their understanding of, and pleasure in, the poems.

Technical terms

In order to enjoy a poem it is not necessary to know that a poet uses metaphor or alliteration. But to talk about and interpret poetry, students will need a basic knowledge of such technical terms. They are the language of criticism and students should be taught how to use them so that they become helpful in closer analysis of individual poems. Overloading students with terminology, however, will lead only to confusion or boredom. The poems themselves will provide the best context for introducing these terms, and terminology has been explained and highlighted in the questions. The glossary at the back of the book will be a useful check-list, and the page number refers back to the original definition.

The structure of this anthology

Grouping the poems

The poems in this anthology have been grouped along thematic lines and each of the seven sections has been given a title taken from lines in one of the poems it covers. The sections have been chosen to reflect the range of experience of young people growing up in Africa today. In *a different heartbeat* are poems about **love**; *charting my own futures* is about finding a sense of **identity**; *the mourning song* tells of **death**; different aspects of **village life** are reflected in *on the earthen floor*; *Song of exile* includes poems of **separation**; in *he who owns you is among you here*, the poetry explores **power**, and the anthology ends with a section on **freedom** poems: *leading us towards sunrise*.

The poems have not necessarily been arranged in order of difficulty; the arrangement within sections is more closely linked to the ideas within the poems, so that poems which share a point of view or, perhaps, present a contrasting picture are placed near each other. The poems can be read in groups or taken separately: each poem is both an individual work and a part of a wider frame of observation on life. The way you use this anthology is a matter of personal choice; there is certainly no need to work through each section from beginning to end.

The questions

The questions are not intended to be prescriptive or to suggest authoritative interpretations. They are provided to support both you, the teacher, and your students in being able to get the maximum out of a poem. The questions are of three types:

1 Before you read

General activities to draw out students' feelings and experiences. These are included at the beginning of each section and relate to the particular theme. They are intended to be considered before students read the poems, but the choice of which or how many to tackle is yours. In one or two cases a particular poem is presented in a different and specially structured way for students to consider *before* they read the actual poem.

2 *After you read*

General questions based on a reading of a single or several poems in a section. Again these relate to the theme, but will draw out students' responses to the poems. These are included at the back of the book.

3 *A closer look*

Specific and more detailed questions on selected poems. Students may need to be guided through some of these poems which may have been chosen because they enable students to focus on a particular aspect of poetry: a particular use of language, the use of metaphor or simile, an ironic tone, etc. These detailed questions are also found at the end of the book.

All that has been said here is intended to make poetry pleasurable to you and your students. The experience of poetry should be a sharing one. Poems come alive when they are read aloud and read well. Encourage your students to develop the skill of *listening* to poetry as well as reading it and writing it. After all, poetry is an oral skill, and an important part of the oral tradition of Africa. Writing it down is only a way of making it more permanent. Listening to a poem should be an active learning process, not simply a passive exercise: many of the activities suggested include reading the poems aloud, dramatising them and appreciating the sounds of the poetry as well as its meaning. You will see that there is also an emphasis on talking about the poems: this is because discussing feelings and sharing thoughts after reading a poem helps students to develop their responses to different kinds of poetry. Finally, encourage your students to write poetry themselves, to experiment with language, imagery, form and style, to draft and redraft their work until it says what they want to say.

After all, in our classrooms today are the poets of tomorrow . . .

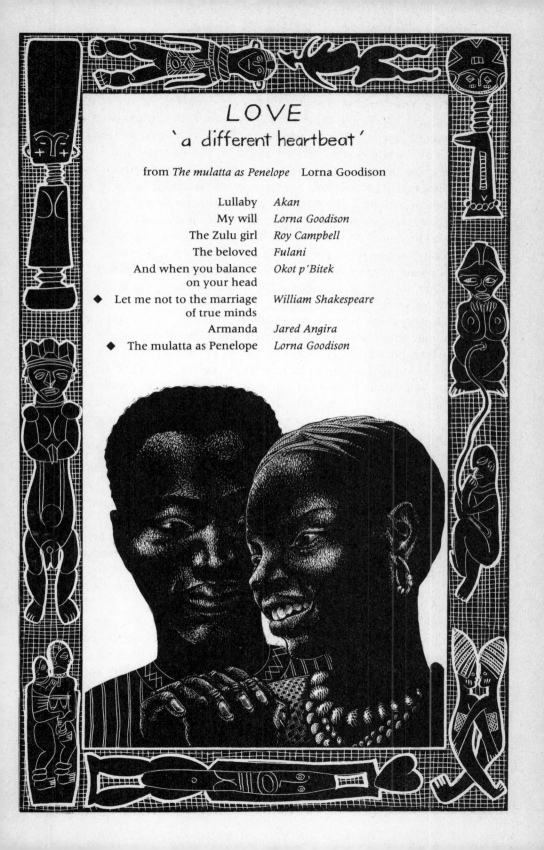

LOVE
`a different heartbeat´

from *The mulatta as Penelope*   Lorna Goodison

Before reading

In this section we have chosen a number of poems about different
sorts of love. Of course, there are poems about love in other parts
of the book: love of your country, love of ideas, love of traditions,
and so on, but the poems here are about love between people.
Lullaby, *The Zulu girl* and *My will* are about the first and perhaps
most important love anyone experiences: the intense feelings of a
mother for her child. The next two poems, *The beloved* and *And
when you balance on your head* reflect men's admiration of the
physical beauty of African women. The last three poems look at
what can happen when people love each other: Shakespeare's
poem *Let me not to the marriage of true minds* explores the idea that
love does not alter; *Armanda* and *The mulatta as Penelope* look at
how it feels when love does change.

1 As a class, think about as many different sorts of love as you can.
   Call out your ideas to your teacher who will write them down on
   the blackboard. You will have two minutes for this. Don't
   comment on each other's ideas at this stage. By the end of the
   time you should have quite a long and varied list. This is called
   'brainstorming': it is a good way of sharing your thoughts and
   gathering lots of ideas quickly. Now talk about your list and sort
   it out into different groups, such as 'the love between two
   adults', 'the love between adults and children', 'love for things',
   etc.

2 Which sort of love do you expect love poems to be written
   about? Can you think of any examples? (Don't forget that love
   songs are also love poems.)
   Are there any particular words or ideas that often appear in love
   poems? List any that you can think of and after you have read all
   the poems refer back to your notes for your own interest. You
   might find it easier to do this in small groups of two or three and
   then compare your ideas with the rest of the class.

3 Some of the poems in this section are about the love that men
   and women have for each other and the loss of that love. Do you
   expect there to be any differences in the way men and women
   describe their feelings? What differences might you expect? You
   could discuss this idea in small groups and then see if you were
   right about any differences when you have read the poems.

Lullaby

Someone would like to have you for her child
but you are mine.
Someone would like to rear you on a costly mat
but you are mine.
Someone would like to place you on a camel blanket
but you are mine.
I have you to rear on a torn old mat.
Someone would like to have you as her child
but you are mine.

Akan (Ghana)

My will

Son, my will,
albeit premature
when the palm readers
divine
for me an extended
life line.

Besides who knows what
worth bequeathing
I could acquire
before the life line
inches to the darker side
of my hand.

But, for a start,
the gift of song,
this sweet immediate source
of release was not given me
so I leave it for you in the hope
that God takes hints.

Then the right to call
all older than you
Miss, mister or mistress
in the layered love of our
simplest ways,
eat each day's salt and bread
with praise,
and may you never know hungry
And books
I mean the love of them.

May you like me earn good
friends
but just to be sure,
love books.
When bindings fall apart
they can be fixed
you will find
that is not always so
with friendships.
And no gold.
Too many die/kill for it
besides its face is too bold.
This observation is the
last I give:
most times assume a
patina a shade subdued
so when you bloom they
will value it.

Lorna Goodison (Jamaica)

The Zulu girl

When in the sun the hot red acres smoulder,
Down where the sweating gang its labour plies,
A girl flings down her hoe, and from her shoulder
Unslings her child tormented by the flies.

She takes him to a ring of shadow pooled
By thorn-trees: purpled with the blood of ticks,
While her sharp nails, in slow caresses ruled,
Prowl through his hair with sharp electric clicks.

His sleepy mouth plugged by the heavy nipple,
Tugs like a puppy, grunting as he feeds:
Through his frail nerves her own deep languors ripple
Like a broad river sighing through its reeds.

Yet in that drowsy stream his flesh imbibes
An old unquenched unsmotherable heat –
The curbed ferocity of beaten tribes,
The sullen dignity of their defeat.

Her body looms above him like a hill
Within whose shade a village lies at rest,
Or the first cloud so terrible and still
That bears the coming harvest in its breast.

Roy Campbell (S. Africa)

The beloved

Diko,
of light skin, of smooth hair and long;
her smell is sweet and gentle
she never stinks of fish
she never breathes sweat
like gatherers of dry wood.
She has no bald patch on her head
like those who carry heavy loads.
Her teeth are white
her eyes are like
those of a new born fawn
that delights in the milk
that flows for the first time
from the antelope's udder.

Neither her heel nor her palm
are rough; but sweet to touch
like liver; or better still
the fluffy down of kapok.

Fulani (Nigeria)

And when you balance on your head

And when you balance on your head
A beautiful water pot
Or a new basket
Or a long-necked jar
Full of Honey,
Your long neck
Resembles the alwiri spear

And as you walk along the pathway,
On both sides
The abiya grasses are flowering
And the pollok blossoms
And the wild white lilies
Are shouting silently
To the bees and butterflies!

And as the fragrance
Of the ripe wild berries
Hooks the insects and little birds,
As the fishermen hook the fish
And pull them up mercilessly,
The young men come
From the surrounding villages,
And from across many streams,
They come from beyond the hills
And the wide plains.
They surround you
And bite off their ears
Like jackals.

And when you go
To the well
Or into the freshly burnt woodlands
To collect the red oceyu
Or to cut oduggu shrubs,
You find them
Lurking in the shades
Like the leopardess with cubs.

from Song of Lawino by Okot p'Bitek (Uganda)

◆ Let me not to the marriage of true minds

Let me not to the marriage of true minds
Admit impediments. Love is not love
Which alters when it alteration finds,
Or bends with the remover to remove:
O, no! it is an ever-fixed mark,
That looks on tempests and is never shaken;
It is the star to every wandering bark,
Whose worth's unknown, although his height be taken.
Love's not Time's fool, though rosy lips and cheeks
Within his bending sickle's compass come;
Love alters not with his brief hours and weeks,
But bears it out even to the edge of doom.
    If this be error, and upon me prov'd,
    I never writ, nor no man ever lov'd.

William Shakespeare (England)

Armanda

Armanda was a well-meaning lass:
Read anthropology at college,
Danced the tango quite a lot
Drank the whisky on the rocks,

Smoked Dunhill to the hills
And drove men off their heads
By her beauty, the beauty of the peahen.

Armanda was a well-meaning lass:
Hated the kitchen and its bureaucracy,
Abhorred the cards and the bridge,
Disliked the chess and the radio,
Screamed at the telly,
And frowned at the Scrabble.

Armanda was a well-meaning lass
Until she turned the apple-cart
Marrying the semi-paralytic Ray;
That was 'true love', so she said
And insisted that the crutches
Were part of Ray that sent her on heart
And tickled her most!

Armanda was a well-meaning lass
Until they flew to distant lands
To sow the seeds of *happiness*;
In her well meaning, thank God,
There is hell expanding each day.
She led him to the bank
Laying all the millions
Into Armanda who missed nothing
And misses nobody.

In her well meaning, thank heavens,
There is hell, heating each day.
She led him to the orthopaedics
Recommending a plastic thigh.
Henceforth, Ray too could dance the tango
And converse at cocktail parties
All without the 'tickling' crutches.

There is no perfection in this world:
The surgery a disaster,
Ray regressed to the wheelchair

And Armanda confined to sympathy.
The well-meaning eyes went shy
And the sight of love
Became the sight of pity.
Safe with the account,
Safe with the pills,
Suddenly she qualified as judge
To judge the quick and the slow.

Life between two people
Is but plastic association
When one is resigned to pity
When one must always give
And another ever receive,
If I must dress you up
And push your wheelchair,
You too must dress me up
And drive me to the beach
A meaningful marriage.

One evening as the wind blew
A piece of paper came floating
In the wind and as it rested on Ray's lap
He read what he had always expected one day,

　　　'Goodbye love, goodbye Ray,
　　　I thought I could change it
　　　But I have failed
　　　And I've flown home'

And Ray never thought
Of his millions in her name.

Jared Angira (Kenya)

The mulatta as Penelope

Tonight I'll pull your limbs through small
soft garments
Your head will part my breasts
and you will hear a different heartbeat.
Today we said the real goodbye, he and I
but this time
I will not sit and spin and spin
the door open to let the madness in
till the sailor finally weary
of the sea
returns with tin souvenirs and a claim
to me.
True, I returned from the quayside
my eyes full of sand
and his salt leaving smell
fresh on my hands
But, you're my anchor awhile now
and that goes deep,
I'll sit in the sun and dry my hair
while you sleep.

Lorna Goodison (Jamaica)

Further questions for this section may be found on page 83.

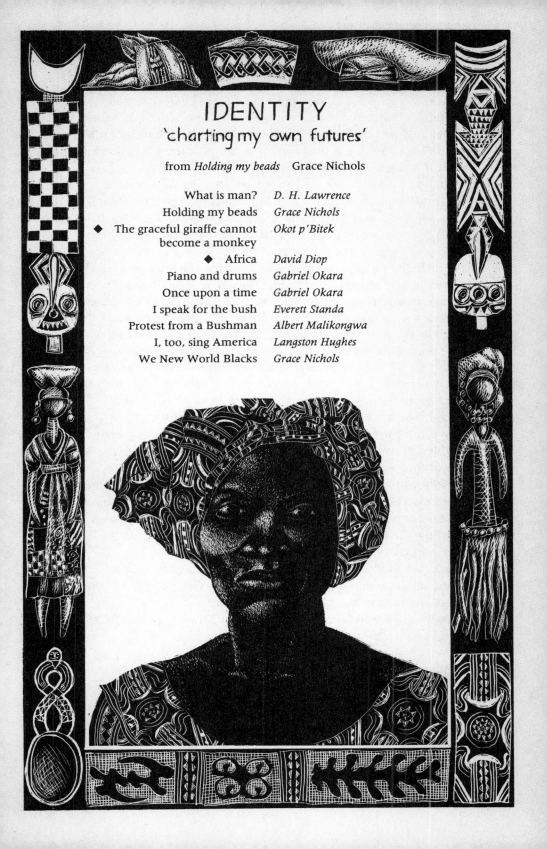

IDENTITY
'charting my own futures'

from *Holding my beads*   Grace Nichols

Before reading

In this section the poets are exploring different kinds of identity: who we are, what makes us what we are, what it is to be us, what we will be if we take control of our own lives. This is a section that speaks directly to young people who are asking themselves these same questions as they grow towards maturity.

When you read the poems you will see that the section starts with some definitions of how people see themselves: *What is man?*, *Holding my beads* and *The graceful giraffe cannot become a monkey*. In these poems the poets explore the qualities that give us our sense of our own identity, the things that define what we are. Then we have included some poems that look at African identity, in a tribal, geographic and historic sense: *Africa, I speak for the bush* and *Protest from a bushman*. The two poems by Gabriel Okara, *Piano and drums* and *Once upon a time*, explore the conflicts within the individual caused by the difference between European and African cultures. These poems lead us outwards from Africa to the 'New World Blacks'; the Africans who have become the Afro-Caribbeans, the Afro-Americans and Afro-Europeans, whose roots still dig down to their African heritage. In *I, too, sing America* and *We New World Blacks* these New World poets, descendants of those who were enslaved long ago and taken to the Americas, are exploring their identities, drawn both from the lands of their birth and from the lands of their ancestors in Africa.

1 Before you start to read the poems, think about what determines your own identity. Do you think it is important that a person has a sense of her or his identity? Make a web like the one opposite to show the things and people that help to shape you into the person that you are and give direction to your life.

2 Discuss the following questions with a partner. (After you have done this, you may want to share your ideas with the rest of the class or you may want to keep them private.)

   a Which of the influences on your life had their greatest effect on you when you were younger?

   b Which affect you most strongly now?

   c What do you think will influence your sense of your own identity in the future?

   d How can 'knowing who you are' help you to take control of your own life?

12

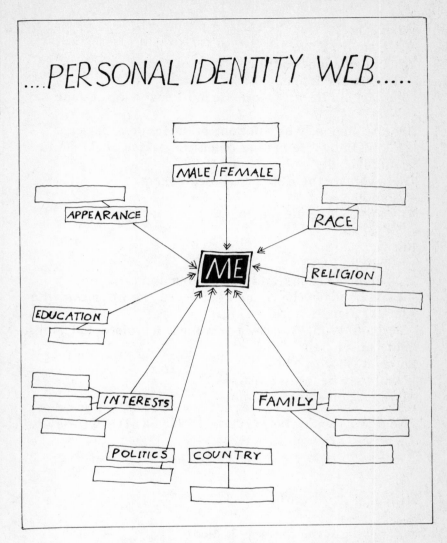

....PERSONAL IDENTITY WEB.....

MALE/FEMALE

APPEARANCE

RACE

ME

RELIGION

EDUCATION

INTERESTS

FAMILY

POLITICS   COUNTRY

3 Have a class discussion about whether you think groups of people, for example in a family or tribe or country or continent, can have a sense of a shared identity. You may want to consider:

a How is a shared identity formed and maintained? How does it change?

b What are the risks for people who are seen to have a group identity?

What is man?

What is he?
— A man, of course.
Yes, but what does he do?
— He lives and is a man.
Oh quite! but he must work. He must have a job of some sort.
— Why?
Because obviously he's not one of the leisured classes.
— I don't know. He has lots of leisure. And he makes quite
beautiful chairs.
There you are then! He's a cabinet maker.
— No no!
Anyhow a carpenter and joiner.
— Not at all
But you said so.
— What did I say?
That he made chairs, and was a joiner and carpenter.
— I said he made chairs, but I did not say he was a carpenter.
All right then, he's just an amateur.
— Perhaps! Would you say a thrush was a professional flautist,
or just an amateur?
I'd say it was just a bird.
— And I say he is just a man.
All right! You always did quibble.

D. H. Lawrence (England)

Holding my beads

Unforgiving as the course of justice
Inerasable as my scars and fate
I am here
a woman . . . . . with all my lives
strung out like beads
                              before me
It isn't privilege or pity
that I seek

It isn't reverence or safety
quick happiness of purity
                    but
the power to be what I am/a woman
charting my own futures/ a woman
holding my beads in my hand

Grace Nichols (Guyana)

◆ The graceful giraffe cannot become a monkey

My husband tells me
I have no ideas
Of modern beauty.
He says
I have stuck
To old-fashioned hair styles.

He says
I am stupid and very backward,
That my hair style
Makes him sick
Because I am dirty.

It is true
I cannot do my hair
As white women do.

Listen,
My father comes from Payira,
My mother is a woman of Koc!
I am a true Acoli
I am not a half-caste
I am not a slave-girl;
My father was not brought home
By the spear
My mother was not exchanged
For a basket of millet.

Ask me what beauty is
To the Acoli
And I will tell you;
I will show it to you
If you give me a chance!

You once saw me,
You saw my hair style
And you admired it,
And the boys loved it.
At the arena
Boys surrounded me
And fought for me.

My mother taught me
Acoli hair fashions;
Which fits the kind
Of hair of the Acoli,
And the occasion.

Listen,
Ostrich plumes differ
From chicken feathers,
A monkey's tail
Is different from that of the giraffe,
The crocodile's skin
Is not like the guinea fowl's,
And the hippo is naked, and hairless.

The hair of the Acoli
Is different from that of the Arabs;
The Indians' hair
Resembles the tail of the horse;
It is like sisal strings
And needs to be cut
With scissors.
It is black,
And is different from that of white women.

A white woman's hair
Is soft like silk;
It is light
And brownish like
That of the brown monkey,
And is very different from mine.
A black woman's hair
Is thick and curly;
It is true
Ring-worm sometimes eats up
A little girl's hair
And this is terrible;
But when hot porridge
Is put on the head
And the dance is held
Under the sausage-fruit tree
And the youths have sung

> *You, Ring-worm*
> *Who is eating Duka's hair*
> *Here is your porridge,*

Then the girl's hair
Begins to grow again
And the girl is pleased.

Okot p'Bitek (Uganda)

◆ Africa

Africa my Africa
Africa of proud warriors in the ancestral savannahs
Africa of whom my grandmother sings
On the banks of the distant river
I have never known you
But your blood flows in my veins
Your beautiful black blood that irrigates the fields
The blood of your sweat

17

The sweat of your work
The work of your slavery
The slavery of your children
Africa tell me Africa
Is this you this back that is bent
This back that breaks under the weight of humiliation
This back trembling with red scars
And saying yes to the whip under the midday sun
But a grave voice answers me
Impetuous son that tree young and strong
That tree there
In splendid loneliness amidst white and faded flowers
That is Africa your Africa
That grows again patiently obstinately
And its fruit gradually acquires
The bitter taste of liberty.

David Diop (Senegal)

Piano and drums

When at break of day at a riverside
I hear jungle drums telegraphing
the mystic rhythm, urgent, raw
like bleeding flesh, speaking of
primal youth and the beginning,
I see the panther ready to pounce,
the leopard snarling about to leap
and the hunters crouch with spears poised;

And my blood ripples, turns torrent,
topples the years and at once I'm
in my mother's lap a suckling;
at once I'm walking simple
paths with no innovations,
rugged, fashioned with the naked
warmth of hurrying feet and groping hearts
in green leaves and wild flowers pulsing.

Then I hear a wailing piano
solo speaking of complex ways
in tear-furrowed concerto;
of far-away lands
and new horizons with
coaxing diminuendo, counterpoint,
crescendo. But lost in the labyrinth
of its complexities, it ends in the middle
of a phrase at a daggerpoint.

And I lost in the morning mist
of an age at a riverside keep
wandering in the mystic rhythm
of jungle drums and the concerto.

Gabriel Okara (Nigeria)

Once upon a time

Once upon a time, son,
they used to laugh with their hearts
and laugh with their eyes;
but now they only laugh with their teeth,
while their ice-block-cold eyes
search behind my shadow.

There was a time indeed
they used to shake hands with their hearts;
but that's gone, son,
Now they shake hands without hearts
while their left hands search
my empty pockets.

'Feel at home,' 'Come again,'
they say, and when I come
again and feel
at home, once, twice,
there will be no thrice —
for then I find doors shut on me.

So I have learned many things, son.
I have learned to wear many faces
like dresses — homeface,
        office face, streetface, hostface, cocktailface,
with all their comforting smiles
like a fixed portrait smile.

And I have learned too
to laugh with only my teeth
and shake hands without my heart.
I have also learned to say 'Goodbye'
when I mean 'Goodriddance';
to say 'Glad to meet you';
without being glad; and to say 'It's been
nice talking to you' after being bored.

But believe me, son
I want to be what I used to be
when I was like you. I want
to unlearn all these muting things.
Most of all, I want to relearn
how to laugh, for my laugh in the mirror
shows only my teeth like a snake's bare fangs!

So show me, son
how to laugh; show me how
I used to laugh and smile
once upon a time when I was like you.

Gabriel Okara (Nigeria)

I speak for the bush

When my friend sees me
He swells and pants like a frog
Because I talk the wisdom of the bush!
He says we from the bush
Do not understand civilized ways

For we tell our women
To keep the hem of their dresses
Below the knee.
We from the bush, my friend insists,
Do not know how to 'enjoy':
When we come to the civilized city,
Like nuns, we stay away from nightclubs
Where women belong to no men
And men belong to no women
And these civilized people
Quarrel and fight like hungry lions!

But, my friend, why do men
With crippled legs, lifeless eyes,
Wooden legs, empty stomachs
Wander about the streets
Of this civilized world?

Teach me, my friend, the trick,
So that my eyes may not
See those whose houses have no walls
But emptiness all around;
Show me the wax you use
To seal your ears
To stop hearing the cry of the hungry;
Teach me the new wisdom
Which tells men
To talk about money and not love,
When they meet women;

Tell your God to convert
Me to the faith of the indifferent,
The faith of those
Who will never listen until
They are shaken with blows.

I speak for the bush:
You speak for the civilized —
Will you hear me?

Everett Standa (Kenya)

Protest from a Bushman

This is my native land
My real native land
I know every tree or bush by its name
I know every bird or beast by its name
I care not that I am poor
I have lived in this land
And hunted all over these mountains
And have looked at the skies
And wondered how the stars
And the moon and the sun and the
Rainbow and the Milky Way rush
From day to day like busy people
I have enjoyed this life
The light in the stars
The lilt in the music or songs
The joy in the flowers
The plumage of the birds
The charm in women's breasts
The inward warmth and rich vitality
The distant music of cowbells
All these lightened the burdens of my sorrow
I have nothing outside this body
I have neither a house nor property
I roamed where I liked and entered where I chose
And have enjoyed the bounce of youth
And stayed where I chose
I have danced in the sun
I have danced in the wind
I have danced around the fire place
But now and I say now there is
A swelling crescendo of sorrow
That makes goose-pimples on my body
There is no more joy in me
I live in sick apprenhension

Albert Malikongwa (Botswana)

I, too, sing America

I, too sing America

I am the darker brother.
They send me to eat in the kitchen
When company comes,
But I laugh,
And eat well,
And grow strong.

Tomorrow,
I'll sit at the table
When company comes.
Nobody'll dare
Say to me,
'Eat in the kitchen',
Then.

Besides,
They'll see how beautiful I am
And be ashamed –

I, too, am, America.

Langston Hughes (USA)

We New World Blacks

The timbre
in our voice
betrays us
however far
we've been

whatever tongue
we speak
the old ghost

asserts itself
in dusky echoes

like driftwood
traces

and in spite of
ourselves
we know the way
back to

the river stone

the little decayed
spirit
of the navel string
hiding in our back garden

Grace Nichols (Guyana)

Further questions for this section may be found on page 86.

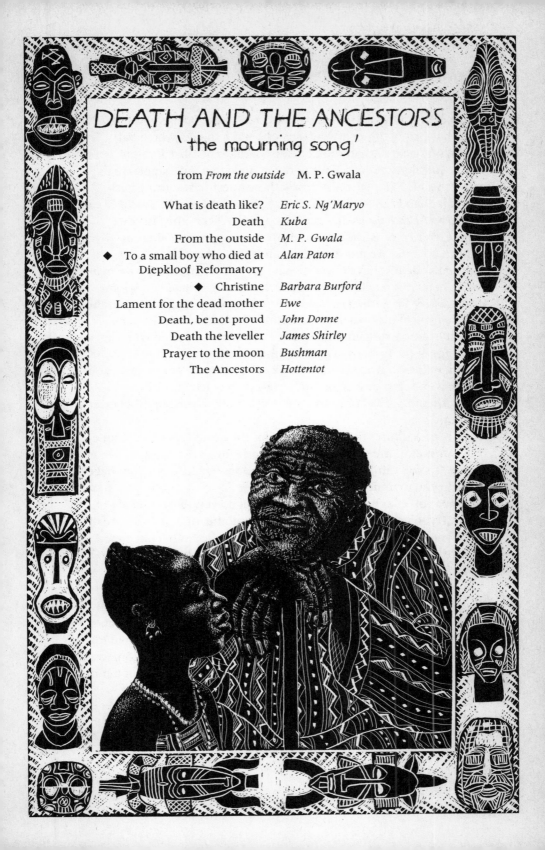

DEATH AND THE ANCESTORS
'the mourning song'

from *From the outside*   M. P. Gwala

Before reading

The poems in this section are 'mourning songs': poems about death. Death is part of our everyday lives and it is a subject which has always fascinated writers and artists, perhaps because it raises two basic questions: what are we here for, and what will happen to us after this life? The poems here ask these questions, starting with *What is death like?*. Some of them are philosophical, like *Death, be not proud* and *Death the leveller* and look at death 'from the outside'. Some, like *Prayer to the moon* and *The Ancestors*, are religious or spiritual. Some are more personal and tell us about the effect particular deaths have on those who are left to grieve, such as *From the outside*, *To a small boy who died at Deipkloof Reformatory*, *Christine* and *Lament for the dead mother*. One of the poems, *Death*, is about the poet's view of his own death and funeral. In many of the poems, death – the passing into the unknown future – is linked with the heritage of the unknown past and the ancestors.

1 What does death make you think of? You could 'brainstorm' your ideas as a class or just jot down your own reactions. Is it frightening or sad or is it a time to celebrate passing on to a better world?

   In some cultures there is a 'wake' for the dead. This can last nine nights; after the wake the period of grieving is over and life can go on. Do you think this is a good idea? Does having a religious belief help you to understand death?

2 Have you ever been to a funeral? What do you remember about it? Try to use all your senses as you recall the funeral. Was it really about death or about life? What did people do? What happened after the funeral? Write a short description of a funeral (real or imagined), and try to describe it so vividly that anyone reading your work will feel that they were there too.

3 Look in a newspaper for an obituary (a tribute to a dead person). What things are said about the dead person in the obituary you have found? What has been put in and what has been left out? Can you tell what sort of person he or she was? Think of someone you know or someone famous and write an obituary about her or him.

What is death like?

What is death like?
Is it like a flash of lightning
Or a clap of thunder
In a night of Storm
Then eternal stillness
And dark?

Is it like a sudden opening
Of a secret door
Like the vaginal opening
To a newly born,
Then colour, variety and —
Life?

What is death like?

Eric S. Ng'Maryo (Tanzania)

Death

There is no needle without piercing point.
There is no razor without trenchant blade.
Death comes to us in many forms.

With our feet we walk the goat's earth.
With our hands we touch God's sky.
Some future day in the heat of noon,
I shall be carried shoulder high
through the village of the dead.
When I die, don't bury me under forest trees,
I fear their thorns.
When I die, don't bury me under forest trees.
I fear the dripping water.
Bury me under the great shade trees in the market,
I want to hear the drums beating
I want to feel the dancers' feet.

Kuba (Sudan)

27

From the outside

We buried Madaza
on a Sunday;
big crowd:
hangarounds, churchgoers,
drunks and goofs;
even the fuzz
were there
as the priest
hurried
the burial sermon –
and we filled the grave
with red soil,
the mourning song
pitched fistedly high;
what got my brow itching though
is that none
of the cops present
dared to stand out and say
Madaza was a 'Wanted'.

M. P. Gwala (S. Africa)

◆ To a small boy who died at Diepkloof Reformatory

Small offender, small innocent child
With no conception or comprehension
Of the vast machinery set in motion
By your trivial transgression,
Of the great forces of authority,
Of judges, magistrates, and lawyers,
Psychologists, psychiatrists, and doctors,
Principals, police, and sociologists,
Kept moving and alive by your delinquency,
This day, and under the shining sun
Do I commit your body to the earth
Oh child, oh lost and lonely one.

Clerks are moved to action by your dying;
Your documents, all neatly put together,
Are transferred from the living to the dead,
Here is the document of birth
Saying that you were born and where and when,
But giving no hint of joy or sorrow,
Or if the sun shone, or if the rain was falling,
Or what bird flew singing over the roof
Where your mother travailed. And here your name
Meaning in white man's tongue, he is arrived
But to what end or purpose is not said.

Here is the last certificate of Death;
Forestalling authority he sets you free,
You that did once arrive have now departed
And are enfolded in the sole embrace
Of kindness that earth ever gave to you.
So negligent in life, in death belatedly
She pours her generous abundance on you
And rains her bounty on the quivering wood
And swaddles you about, where neither hail nor tempest,
Neither wind nor snow nor any heat of sun
Shall now offend you, and the thin cold spears
Of the highveld rain that once so pierced you
In falling on your grave shall press you closer
To the deep repentant heart

Here is the warrant of committal
For this offence, oh small and lonely one,
For this offence in whose commission
Millions of men are in complicity
You are committed. So do I commit you,
Your frail body to the waiting ground,
Your dust to the dust of the veld, —
Fly home-bound soul to the great Judge-President
Who unencumbered by the pressing need
To give society protection, may pass on you
The sentence of the indeterminate compassion.

Alan Paton (S. Africa)

◆ Christine

She was fine till april,
my child in my belly.
First a little mouse-breath
flutter in a body
that still resented her creation.
Then by christmas, love
that slept with
both hands clasped over her
pushes and swirlings.

To the country, to the nuns.
You're going to keep the child,
my dear?
How brave, but perhaps
you'll change your mind.

I hate azaleas, for
as they bloomed, my child faded
within my belly.
Till she was a dead steel ball
inside a walking wild coffin.
And no help.
Not even from her mother
who could not look.
Who listened to love clang
in a kidney-dish with
tight shut eyes.
And asked – What is it?

Providence, said the nuns,
kind providence.
A little girl.
And I don't even know
where she is buried.
Christine,
I hate azaleas.

Barbara Burford (Jamaica)

Lament for the dead mother

Mother dear,
Mother you freely give of what you have
fresh food and cooked meals alike.
Mother, listen to me:
the crying child will call after its mother.
Why don't you answer, Mother, when I call?
Are we quarrelling?

Ewe (Ghana)

Death, be not proud

Death, be not proud, though some have called thee
Mighty and dreadful, for thou art not so;
For those whom thou think'st thou dost overthrow
Die not, poor Death, nor yet canst thou kill me.
From rest and sleep, which but thy pictures be,
Much pleasure — then from thee much more must flow;
And soonest our best men with thee do go,
Rest of their bones and soul's delivery.
Thou art slave to fate, chance, kings and desperate men,
And dost with poison, war, and sickness dwell;
And poppy or charms can make us sleep as well,
And better than thy stroke. Why swell'st thou then?
One short sleep past, we wake eternally,
And death shall be no more. Death, thou shalt die.

John Donne (England)

Death the leveller

The glories of our blood and state
    Are shadows, not substantial things;
There is no armour against Fate;
    Death lays his icy hand on kings:

Sceptre and Crown
Must tumble down,
And in the dust be equal made
With the poor crooked scythe and spade.

Some men with swords may reap the field,
And plant fresh laurels where they kill:
But their strong nerves at last must yield;
They tame but one another still:
Early or late
They stoop to fate,
And must give up the murmuring breath
When they, pale captives, creep to death.

The garlands wither on your brow;
Then boast no more your mighty deeds!
Upon Death's purple altar now
See where the victor-victim bleeds.
Your heads must come,
To the cold tomb:

Only the actions of the just
Smell sweet and blossom in their dust.

James Shirley (England)

Prayer to the moon

Take my face and give me yours!
Take my face, my unhappy face.
Give me your face,
with which you return
when you have died,
when you vanished from sight.
You lie down and return –
Let me reassemble you, because you have joy,
you return evermore alive,

after you vanished from sight.
Did you not promise us once
that we too should return
and be happy again after death?

Bushman (Botswana)

The Ancestors

The days have passed;
we are a wandering camp
brighter days before us
perhaps.

Light fades
night becomes darker.
Hunger tomorrow.

God is angry
the elders have gone.
Their bones are far
their souls wander.
Where are their souls?

The passing wind
knows it perhaps.

Their bones are far
their souls wander.
Are they far away,
are they quite close?
Do they want sacrifice,
do they want blood?
Are they far,
are they near?

The passing wind
the spirit that whirls the leaf
know it perhaps.

Hottentot (S. Africa)

Further questions for this section may be found on page 90.

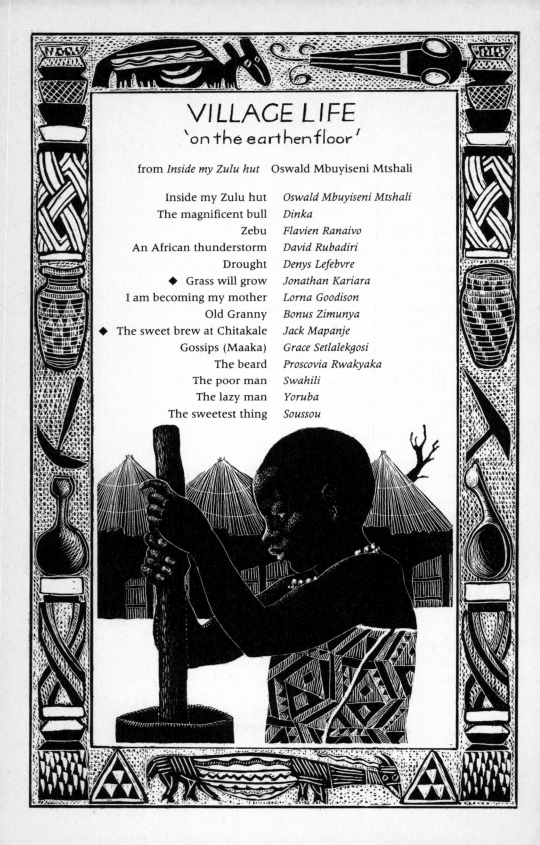

VILLAGE LIFE
'on the earthen floor'

from *Inside my Zulu hut*   Oswald Mbuyiseni Mtshali

Before reading

In this section you will find poems about village life in Africa,
about the people and the animals living 'on the earthen floor' and
closely bound to the forces of nature. The poems are about
everyday life: we start *Inside my Zulu hut*; there are two poems in
praise of animals: *The magnificient bull* and *Zebu* and two about the
extremes of climate: *An African thunderstorm* and *Drought*. The rest
of the poems describe village people: *I am becoming my mother, Old
Granny, The beard, The poor man*; the things they do: *The sweet brew
at Chitakale, Gossips, The lazy man*; and the things that matter to
them: *Grass will grow* and *The sweetest thing*.

The poems have warmth and humour; people's weaknesses are
seen with some sympathy and the power and beauty of nature is
recognised. You will notice that because the poems in this section
are descriptive, they are full of similes and metaphors. These
images make the poems more vivid and express the poets' ideas in
a unique way.

Many of the poems in this section are traditional; they are part
of the body of **oral literature** which is passed down through
generations, not as written texts but as spoken poems taught to
children by their elders. How do you think passing on a poem by
word of mouth rather than on the printed page affects the way it is
shaped? When you read the poems try to find answers to this
question.

1 Try a word association game: start with 'village' and go round
   the class, each adding a word that you associate with 'village'.
2 Read *I speak for the bush* (p. 20) again. Draw two columns and
   head one side VILLAGE LIFE and the other TOWN LIFE. Write the
   differences you find in the poem between town and village life
   in the two columns. You could start like this:

VILLAGE LIFE	TOWN LIFE
women wear long dresses	women wear short skirts
it is important to be faithful	people flirt /are promiscuous

When you have done this, discuss whether you think the
bushman's view is right and add your ideas about town and
village life to the lists.

3 Work in groups of two or three. Write down three images for
each of these words; try to make your similes and metaphors as
original as you can:
     white   black   light   dark   red   green   hot
Then compare your images with the rest of the class.

Inside my Zulu hut

It is a hive
without any bees
to build the walls
with golden bricks of honey.
A cave cluttered
with a millstone,
calabashes of sour milk
claypots of foaming beer
sleeping grass mats
wooden head rests
tanned goat skins
tied with *riempies*
to wattle rafters
blackened by the smoke
of kneaded cow dung
burning under
the three legged pot
on the earthen floor
to cook my porridge

Oswald Mbuyiseni Mtshali (S. Africa)

The magnificent bull

My bull is white like the silver fish in the river
white like the shimmering crane bird on the river bank
white like fresh milk!
His roar is like the thunder to the Turkish
cannon on the steep shore.
My bull is dark like the raincloud in the storm.
He is like summer and winter.
Half of him is dark like the storm cloud,
Half of him is light like sunshine.
His back shines like the morning star.
His brow is red like the beak of the Hornbill.
His forehead is like a flag, calling the people from a distance,
He resembles the rainbow.

I will water him at the river,
With my spear I shall drive my enemies.
Let them water their herds at the well;
The river belongs to me and my bull.
Drink, my bull, from the river; I am here
to guard you with my spear.

Dinka (Sudan)

Zebu

His lips move unceasingly
But they are not swollen or worn;
His teeth are two fine rows of coral;
His horns form a circle
Which is never closed.
His eyes: two immense pearls shining in the night;
His hump is Mount-Abundance
His tail lashes the air
But is not more than half a fly-switch;
His body is a well-filled coffer
On four dry sticks.

Flavien Ranaivo (Madagascar)

An African thunderstorm

From the west
Clouds come hurrying with the wind
Turning
Sharply
Here and there
Like a plague of locusts
Whirling
Tossing up things on its tail
Like a madman chasing nothing.
Pregnant clouds
Ride stately on its back
Gathering to perch on hills
Like dark sinister wings;
The Wind whistles by
And trees bend to let it pass.

In the village
Screams of delighted children
Toss and turn
In the din of the whirling wind.
Women –
Babies clinging on their backs –
Dart about
In and out
Madly
The Wind whirls by
Whilst trees bend to let it pass.
Clothes wave like tattered flags
Flying off
To expose dangling breasts
As jaggered blinding flashes
Rumble, tremble, and crack
Amidst the smell of fired smoke
And the pelting march of the storm.

David Rubadiri (Malawi)

Drought

Heat, all-pervading, crinkles up the soil;
A deathly silence numbs the molten air;
On beds of rivers, islands scorched and bare,
Warm scavengers of wind heap up the spoil;
And wide eyed oxen, gaunt and spent with toil,
Huddled together near some shrunken pool . . .
Pant for the shade of trees and pastures cool,
Lashing their tails at flies they cannot foil.
Whilst overhead, the sun-god drives his way
Through halting hours of blinding, blazing light,
Until his shining steeds a moment stay
And disappear behind the gates of night.
And still, no rain. A cloudless, starlit sky
Watches the veld, and all things droop and die.

Denys Lefebvre (S. Africa)

◆ Grass will grow

If you should take my child Lord
Give my hands strength to dig his grave
cover him with earth
Lord send a little rain
For grass will grow

If my house should burn down
So that the ashes sting the nostrils
Making the eyes weep
The Lord send a little rain
For grass will grow

But Lord do not send me
Madness
I ask for tears
Do not send me moon hard madness
To lodge snug in my skull

I would you sent me hordes of horses
Galloping
Crushing
But do not break
The yolk of the moon on me.

Jonathan Kariara (Kenya)

I am becoming my mother

Yellow/brown woman
fingers smelling always of onions

My mother raises rare blooms
and waters them with tea
her birth waters sang like rivers
my mother is now me

My mother had a linen dress
the colour of the sky
and stored lace and damask
tablecloths
to pull shame out of her eye.

I am becoming my mother
brown/yellow woman
fingers smelling always of onions.

Lorna Goodison (Jamaica)

Old Granny

A little freezing Spider
Legs and arms gathered in her chest
Rocking with flu,
I saw old Granny

At Harare Market;
It was past nine of the night
When I saw the dusty crumpled Spider –
A torn little blanket
Was her web.

Bonus Zimunya (Zimbabwe)

◆ The sweet brew at Chitakale

The old woman squats before a clay jar of *thobwa*
She uncovers the basket lid from the jar and
Stirs attention with a gourdful of the brew.

The customers have all been here: cylists
In dripping sweat have deposited their coins
In the basket gulping down their share,

Pedestrians on various chores have talked
Before the exchange and then cooled their
Parched throats to their money's worth,

But this bus passenger bellows for a gourdful
From the window, drinks deliberately slowly until
The conductor presses the go-button –

The woman picks up the pieces of her broken
Gourd, and dusting her bottom, again squats
Confronting her brew with a borrowed cup.

Jack Mapanje (Malawi)

Gossips (Maaka)

Gossips have neither head nor tail, back nor front
They create a clay cow
until it cries that 'moos' lows
And at sunrise you 'kotela' its calf;

41

its milk fills pails,
that make your children's cheeks glister

Dipotso came out with the words last night
When meeting her on the road.
Mpho clapped her thigh
'I want to know since when Molefi
became my lover'.
The entanglement of words was brought about by whoever;
whoever had caught them, as they flew, from so and so;
so and so had heard them from such and such
who had been whispered to by guess who?

Gossip is the 'diketo' of females
A game with which they distract themselves
Men's talk makes them impatient
They are the ones who want to tatter
a man who gossips smells to them like a skunk

Grace Setalekgosi (Botswana)

translated from Setswana

The beard

In the pulpit he swayed and turned.
Leant forward, backward,
To the right: to the left.
His solemn voice echoed;
Lowly the congregation followed,
'Do you love your neighbour?'
Meekly they bow at his keen eye
Now examining a grey head
Heaving under her sobs.
His heart leapt assured —
'Her sins weigh on her!'
So with her he chats outside;
'Weep not child you are pardoned.'
'But sir, your beard conjured up
The spirit of my dead goat!'

Proscovia Rwakyaka (Uganda)

The poor man

The poor man knows not how to eat with the rich man.
When they eat fish, he eats the head.

Invite a poor man and he rushes in
licking his lips and upsetting the plates.

The poor man has no manners, he comes along
with the blood of lice under his nails.

The face of a poor man is lined
from hunger and thirst in his belly.

Poverty is no state for any mortal man.
It makes him a beast to be fed on grass.

Poverty is unjust. If it befalls a man,
though he is nobly born, he has no power with God.

Swahili (Kenya/Tanzania)

The lazy man

When the cock crows,
the lazy man smacks his lips and says:
So it is daylight again, is it?
And before he turns over heavily,
before he even stretches himself,
before he even yawns —
the farmer has reached the farm,
the water carriers arrive at the river,
the spinners are spinning their cotton,
the weaver works on his cloth,
and the fire blazes in the blacksmith's hut.

The lazy one knows where the soup is sweet
he goes from house to house.

43

If there is no sacrifice today,
his breastbone will stick out!

But when he sees the free yam,
he starts to unbutton his shirt,
he moves close to the celebrant.

Yet his troubles are not few.
When his wives reach puberty,
rich men will help him to marry them.

Yoruba (Nigeria)

The sweetest thing

There is in this world something
that surpasses all other things
in sweetness.
It is sweeter than honey
it is sweeter than salt
it is sweeter than sugar
is it sweeter than all
existing things.
This thing is sleep.
When you are conquered by sleep
nothing can ever prevent you
nothing can stop you from sleeping.
When you are conquered by sleep
and numerous millions arrive
millions arrive to disturb you
millions will find you asleep.

Soussou

Further questions for this section may be found on page 95.

SEPARATION
'song of exile'

from *Yet another song*   David Rubadiri

Before reading

The poems in this section are about separation, the sense of
isolation of those who are away from people whom they love and
places where their 'roots' are. Sometimes the characters in the
poems are unwilling exiles such as in *Letters from a contract worker*,
Refugee Blues, *Life is tremulous* and *Yet another song*. In other poems,
like *Thoughts after work* and *The renegade* the characters have chosen
to leave their origins behind and yet cannot forget them.

Many of these poems are about conflicts inside people. The poets
comment both on the feelings of those who are separated and on
the world we live in which allows (and, indeed, causes) division
and suffering. *The train* and *Footpath*, for example, are about
children's experiences of isolation and the misery it causes. One of
the poems, *Epilogue*, is about separation from one's roots caused by
both time and space, but it is also about a new beginning: a sort of
regrowth from the old root.

Many of the poems in other sections of this anthology could
have been included here: there are so many reasons for separation.
You might like to look at the sections *'Death and the ancestors'* and
'Identity' again and find further examples.

1 Think back to when you were younger. Did you ever get lost in
a busy street or market or in the fields? Do you remember how
you felt? Did the person you got separated from tell you how
she or he felt?

Work in pairs to make a poem for two voices about a parent
and child being separated and reunited. First, decide in what sort
of place the separation happens. Then work separately for a little
while: one person should write the thoughts of the child and the
other person should write the thoughts of the mother or father.
Use your own feelings and experiences to help you. You don't
have to use rhyme or have a regular pattern, but your ideas
should be written in lines like a poem. When you put your ideas
together, you may want to have alternate lines spoken by the
parent and the child, or you may want to have a group of lines
spoken by one and then the other. Try saying your poem aloud
and make it as dramatic as you can. When you are satisfied with
it, say it to the rest of the class.

2 What causes people to leave people and places they love? Work in small groups and make a list of your ideas. Then put the lists together into a class list. Discuss the reasons you find: which of them are connected with a personal choice and which of them are caused by factors outside the individual's control? Sort the list into two groups under the headings CHOSE TO GO and FORCED TO GO. Some of your ideas may go into both lists. Keep your lists.
3 Have you ever read a story about a separation? Write a short review of the story or tell the class the story and explain why you remember it.

Letter from a contract worker

I wanted to write you a letter
my love,
a letter that would tell
of this desire
to see you
of this fear
of losing you
of this more than benevolence that I feel
of this indefinable ill that pursues me
of this yearning to which I live in total surrender . . .

I wanted to write you a letter
my love
a letter of intimate secrets,
a letter of memories of you,
of you
of your lips red as henna
of your hair black as mud
of your eyes sweet as honey
of your breasts hard as wild orange
or your lynx gait.
and of your caresses
such that I can find no better here . . .

47

I wanted to write you a letter
my love
that would recall the days in our haunts
our nights lost in the long grass
that would recall the shade falling on us from the plum
trees
the moon filtering through the endless palm trees
that would recall the madness
of our passion
and the bitterness
of our separation . . .

I wanted to write you a letter
my love
that you would not read without sighing
that you would hide from papa Bombo
that you would withhold from mama Kieza
that you would reread without the coldness
of forgetting
a letter to which in all Kilombo
no other would stand comparison . . .

I wanted to write a letter
my love
a letter that would be brought to you by the passing wind
a letter that the cashews and coffee trees,
the hyenas and buffaloes
the alligators and grayling
could understand
so that if the wind should lose it on the way
the beasts and plants
with pity for our sharp suffering
from song to song
lament to lament
gabble to gabble
would bring you pure and hot
the burning words
the sorrowful words of the letter
I wanted to write to you my love . . .

I wanted to write you a letter . . .

But oh my love, I cannot understand
why it is, why it is, why it is my dear,
that you cannot read
and I — oh the hopelessness! — cannot write

Antonio Jacinto (Angola)

Translated from the Portuguese

Refugee Blues

Say this city has ten million souls,
Some are living in mansions, some are living in holes:
Yet there's no place for us, my dear, yet there's no place
for us.

Once we had a country and we thought it fair,
Look in the atlas and you'll find it there:
We cannot go there now, my dear, we cannot go there now.

In the village churchyard there grows an old yew,
Every spring it blossoms anew:
Old passports can't do that, my dear, old passports can't
do that.

The consul banged the table and said,
'If you've got no passport you're officially dead':
But we are still alive, my dear, but we are still alive.

Went to a committee; they offered me a chair;
Asked me politely to return next year:
But where shall we go to-day, my dear, where shall we
go to-day?

Came to a public meeting; the speaker got up and said:
'If we let them in, they will steal our daily bread':
He was talking of you and me, my dear, he was talking
of you and me.

t I heard the thunder rumbling in the sky;
Iitler over Europe, saying, 'They must die':
rere in his mind, my dear, O we were in his mind.

Saw a poodle in a jacket fastened with a pin,
Saw a door opened and a cat let in:
But they weren't German Jews, my dear, but they
    weren't German Jews.

Went down the harbour and stood upon the quay,
Saw the fish swimming as if they were free:
Only ten feet away, my dear, only ten feet away.

Walked through a wood, saw the birds in the trees;
They had no politicians and sang at their ease:
They weren't the human race, my dear, they weren't
    the human race.

Dreamed I saw a building with a thousand floors,
A thousand windows and a thousand doors:
Not one of them was ours, my dear, not one of them was
    ours.

Stood on a great plain in the falling snow;
Ten thousand soldiers marched to and fro:
Looking for you and me, my dear, looking for you and me.

W. H. Auden (England)

◆ Epilogue

I have crossed an ocean
I have lost my tongue
from the root of the old
one
a new one has sprung

Grace Nichols (Guyana)

The train

The train
carries everybody
everywhere.

It carries the men
It carries the women
It carries me too
a blind boy.
Wherever it carries me
alas, I meet distress
and knock against it
with my knee.
It carries the men
It carries the women
It carries the blind boy
to his distress.

Iteso (Uganda)

Life is tremulous

Life is tremulous like a waterdrop on a mophane tree
My body is wrinkled, my hair grey
The talk is Bushmen everywhere
I am called a 'no body'
A race of ragged filthy people
Who cannot clean their floors
Whose blanket is the firewood
Who spit and sneeze freely everywhere
Whose bodies smell of root-ointment
Or like a cowhide soaked in the river water
My countrymen call me names
I am torn between life and death
Propped between freedom and slavery
My tears glide in pairs down my cheeks
My hands shake because of old age

I am no more than a refugee
A loafer they say
Yet others loaf too whilst other men work
It is true I do not worry for lunch
As birds do not worry for theirs too
To me the delights of knowledge
And the pomp of power are anathema
Life is tremulous like drops
Of water on a mophane leaf
My countrymen eat, drink and laugh
I and my fellow men and women sleep under trees
In caves or open ground
We starve, we can no longer hunt freely
Life is a scourge, a curse
It is tremulous like a drop of water on a mophane leaf.

Albert G. T. K. Malikongwa (Botswana)

Footpath

Path-let . . . leaving home, leading out,
Return my mother to me.
The sun is sinking and darkness coming.
Hens and cocks are already inside and babies
    drowsing,
Return my mother to me.
We do not have firewood and I have not seen the
    lantern,
There is no more food and the water has run out,
Path-let I pray you, return my mother to me.
Path of the hillocks, path of the small stones,
Path of slipperiness, path of the mud,
Return my mother to me.
Path of the papyrus, path of the rivers.
Path of the small forests, path of the reeds,
Return my mother to me.
Path that winds, path of the short cut,
Over-trodden path, newly made path,

Return my mother to me.
Path, I implore you, return my mother to me.
Path of the crossways, path that branches off,
Path of the stinging shrubs, path of the bridge,
Return my mother to me.
Path of the open, path of the valley,
Path of the steep climb, path of the downward slope,
Return my mother to me.
Children are drowsing, about to sleep,
Darkness is coming and there is no firewood,
And I have not found the lantern:
Return my mother to me.

Stella Ngatho (Uganda)

Thoughts after work

Clear laughter of African children
Rings loud in the evening:
Here around this musty village
Evening falls like a mantle,
Gracing in all a shroud of peace.
Heavily from my office
I walk
To my village,
My brick government compound,
To my new exile.
In this other compound
I would no longer intrude.
I perch over a chasm,
Ride a storm I cannot hold,
And so must pass on quietly –
The laughter of children rings loud
Bringing back to me
Simple joys I once knew.

David Rubadiri (Malawi)

The renegade

My brother you flash your teeth in response to every hypocrisy
My brother with gold-rimmed glasses
You give your master a blue-eyed faithful look
My poor brother in immaculate evening dress
Screaming and whispering and pleading in the parlours of
condescension
We pity you
Your country's burning sun is nothing but a shadow
On your serene 'civilized' brow
And the thought of your grandmother's hut
Brings blushes to your face that is bleached
By years of humiliation and bad conscience
And while you trample on the bitter red soil of Africa
Let these words of anguish keep time with your restless step –
Oh I am lonely so lonely here.

David Diop (Senegal)

Yet another song

Yet another song
I have to sing:
In the early wake
Of a colonial dusk
I sang the song of fire.

The church doors opened
To the clang
of new anthems
And colourful banners.

Like the Beatles,
The evangelical hymns
of conversion
Rocked the world and me.

I knelt before the new totems
I had helped to raise,
Watered them
With tears of ecstasy.

They grew
Taller than life,
Grimacing and breathing fire.

Today
I sing yet another song
A song of exile.

David Rubadiri (Malawi)

Further questions for this section may be found on page 99.

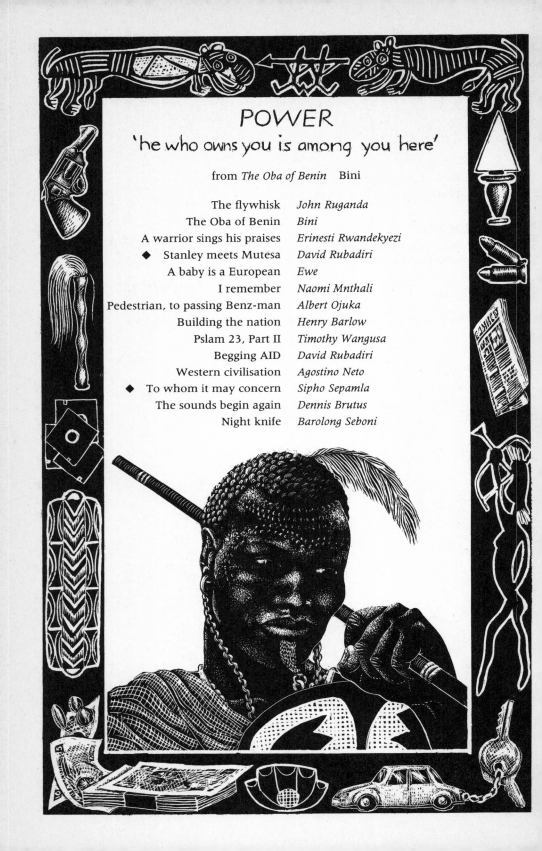

POWER

'he who owns you is among you here'

from *The Oba of Benin*   Bini

Before reading

In this section we explore some ideas about power, the way it can be used, its effects on those who have it and on those whom they control: 'he who owns you is among you here'. We start with three poems which remind us about the strength and power of the ancient rulers of Africa: *The flywhisk, The Oba of Benin* and *A warrior sings his praises*.

The following poems introduce the Europeans: *Stanley meets Mutesa*; and draw ironic comparisons: *A baby is a European*. The next five poems explore the results of the European colonisation of Africa. *I remember* contrasts the past and the present. *Pedestrian, to passing Benz-man, Building the nation* and *Psalm 23, Part II* show the effects of colonialism as Africans copy the patterns of the Europeans despite the ill effects on their own people. *Begging AID* and *Western civilisation* describe how, in some parts of the continent, Africans still have little control over their own lives and the last three poems look very specifically at conditions for black people in South Africa.

1 In groups of two or three, decide what you understand by the word 'power'. Write your definition and then compare it with others in the class. Check your definition with the dictionary and discuss any differences.

2 Who has power over you? Brainstorm all the sorts of power you can think of that affect you own life: for example, your parents or guardians have control over you because of their age and relationship to you and the responsibility they take for your care.

   Who else has power over your life? Remember that sometimes controls over your life are obvious, like school rules. Sometimes they are not so obvious, like having no choice about what you can buy, perhaps because you are too poor to afford better quality. In small groups discuss the different sorts of controls that exist over your lives.

3 What power do you think you have yourself? You may think about people whom you can affect or choices that you can make or things that you can do.

   If you were to become the prime minister or president of your country, what would you use your power then to do? Write an essay on what you would do, and what you would have to consider.

The flywhisk

Fling it sharply, and growl:
Rebels hide their heads
Wave it gently, and smile:
Flies flit from pus drooping eyes
Sling it on the arm, finally:
Empty stomachs will drum for you.

John Ruganda (Uganda)

The Oba of Benin

He who knows not the Oba
Let me show him.
He has mounted the throne,
he has piled a throne upon a throne.
Plentiful as grains of sand on the earth
are those in front of him.
Plentiful as grains of sand on the earth
are those behind him.
There are two thousand people
to fan him.
He who owns you
is among you here.
He who owns you
has piled a throne upon a throne.
He has lived to do it this year;
even so he will live to do it again.

Bini (Nigeria)

A warrior sings his praises

I Who Am Praised thus held out in battle among foreigners
    along with The Overthrower;
I Who Ravish Spear In Each Hand stood out resplendent in
    my cotton cloth;
I Who Am Quick was drawn from afar by lust for the fight
    and with me was The Repulser Of Warriors;
I Who Encircle The Foe, with Bitembe, brought back the
    beasts from Bihanga;
With Bwakwakwa, I fought at Kaanyabareega,
Where Bantura started a song that we might overcome
    them.

Thus with my spear, I and Rwamujonjo conquered
    Oruhinda;
The Banyoro were afraid on the battlefield of Kahenda;
The cocks of Karembe had already crowed;
I Who Am Nimble with The One Whom None Can
    Dislodge felled them at Nyamizi.

At Nkanga, I seized my spear by its shaft-end;
At Kanyegyero, I The Binder Of Enemies took them by
    surprise;
Thereafter was I never excluded from the counsels of
    princes, nor was Rwangomani;
I Who Rescue With The Spear had seized him so that we
    might fight together.

Erinesti Rwandekyezi (Uganda)

◆ Stanley meets Mutesa

Such a time of it they had;
The heat of the day
The chill of the night
And the mosquitoes that followed.
Such was the time and
They bound for a kingdom.

The thin weary line of carriers
With tattered dirty rags to cover their backs;
The battered bulky chests
That kept on falling off their shaven heads.
Their temper high and hot
The sun fierce and scorching
With it rose their spirits
With its fall their hopes
As each day sweated their bodies dry and
Flies clung in clumps on their sweat-scented backs.
Such was the march
And the hot season just breaking.

Each day a weary pony dropped,
Left for the vultures on the plains;
Each afternoon a human skeleton collapsed,
Left for the Masai on the plains;
But the march trudged on
Its Khaki leader in front
He the spirit that inspired.
He the light of hope.

Then came the afternoon of a hungry march,
A hot and hungry march it was;
The Nile and the Nyanza
Lay like two twins
Azure across the green countryside
The march leapt on chaunting
Like young gazelles to a water hole.
Hearts beat faster
Loads felt lighter
As the cool water lapt their sore soft feet.
No more the dread of hungry hyenas
But only tales of valour when
At Mutesa's court fires are lit.
No more the burning heat of the day
But song, laughter and dance.

The village looks on behind banana groves,
Children peer behind reed fences.

Such was the welcome
No singing women to chaunt a welcome
Or drums to greet the white ambassador;
Only a few silent nods from aged faces
And one rumbling drum roll
To summon Mutesa's court to parley
For the country was not sure.

The gate of reeds is flung open,
There is silence
But only a moment's silence –
A silence of assessment.
The tall black king steps forward,
He towers over the thin bearded white man
Then grabbing his lean white hand
Manages to whisper
'Mtu Mweupe karibu'
White man you are welcome.
The gate of polished reeds closes behind them
And the west is let in.

David Rubadiri (Malawi)

A baby is a European

A baby is a European
he does not eat our food:
he drinks from his own water pot.

A baby is a European
He does not speak our tongue:
he is cross when the mother understands him not.

A baby is a European
he cares very little for others:
he forces his will upon his parents.

A baby is a European
He is always very sensitive:
the slightest scratch on his skin results in an ulcer.

Ewe (Togo)

I remember

I remember, Countrymen,
The days of 'Dawn Over the Land'.
Of hopes and expectations
When I truly understood
Slavery was a thing of the past –
We, the people of the land,
Had been freed.
I was there when slowly
Darkness set in.
The gradual destruction
Was there in front of me,
But I did not see it.
I continued, Countrymen, to live in the past.
And when I finally looked
It was too late, and even I
Had become a scavenger.

Naomi Mnthali (Malawi)

Pedestrian, to passing Benz-man

You man, lifted gently
out of the poverty and suffering
We so recently shared; I say –
why splash the muddy puddle on to
my bare legs, as if, still unsatisfied
with your seated opulence
you must sully the unwashed

with your diesel-smoke and mud-water
and force him buy, beyond his means
a bar of soap from your shop?
a few years back we shared a master
today you have none, while I have
exchanged a parasite for something worse.
But maybe a few years is too long a time.

Albert Ojuka (Kenya)

Building the nation

Today I did my share
In building the nation.
I drove a Permanent Secretary
To an important urgent function
In fact to a luncheon at the Vic.

The menu reflected its importance
Cold Bell beer with small talk,
Then fried chicken with niceties
Wine to fill the hollowness of the laughs
Ice-cream to cover the stereotype jokes
Coffee to keep the PS awake on return journey.

I drove the Permanent Secretary back.
He yawned many times in back of the car
Then to keep awake, he suddenly asked,
Did you have any lunch friend?
I replied looking straight ahead
And secretly smiling at his belated concern
That I had not, but was slimming!

Upon which he said with a seriousness
That amused more than annoyed me,
Mwananchi, I too had none!
I attended to matters of state.
Highly delicate diplomatic duties you know,

And friend, it goes against my grain,
Causes me stomach ulcers and wind.
Ah, he continued, yawning again,
The pains we suffer in building the nation!
So the PS had ulcers too!
My ulcers I think are equally painful
Only they are caused by hunger,
No sumptuous lunches!

So two nation builders
Arrived home this evening
With terrible stomach pains
The result of building the nation –
– Different ways.

Henry Barlow (Uganda)

Psalm 23, Part II

The State is my shepherd, I shall not want; it makes me to
    lie down in a subsidized house.
It leads me into political tranquility; it restores my
    faith in a lucrative future.
It leads me into paths of loans and pensions, for its
    international reputation's sake.
Yea, even though I walk through the valley of the shadow
    of Kivvulu I will fear no Kondos;
For the State is with me, its tanks and guns comfort me.
It preserves for me a bank account, in the presence of
    devaluation;
It fills my pocket with allowances, my salary overflows.
Surely increments and promotion shall follow me all the
    days of my life;
And I shall dwell in senior staff quarters for ever.

Timothy Wangusa (Uganda)

Begging AID

Whilst our children
become smaller than guns,
Elders become big
Circus Lions
away from home.
Whilst the manes age
in the Zoos
that now our homelands
have become,
Markets of leftovers
    Guns are taller
    than our children.

In the beggarhood
of a Circus
that now is home,
the whip of the Ringmaster
cracks with a snap
that eats through
the backs of our being.

Hands stretching
in prayer
of submission
in a beggarhood
of Elders delicately
performing the tightrope
to amuse the Gate
for Tips
that will bring home
Toys of death.

David Rubadiri (Malawi)

Western civilisation

Sheets of tin nailed to posts
driven in the ground
make up the house.

Some rags complete
the intimate landscape.

The sun slanting through cracks
welcomes the owner

After twelve hours of slave
labour.
breaking rock
shifting rock
breaking rock
shifting rock
fair weather
wet weather
breaking rock
shifting rock

Old age comes early

a mat on dark nights
is enough when he dies
gratefully
of hunger.

Agostinho Neto (Angola)

Translated from Portuguese by Margaret Dickinson

◆ To whom it may concern

Bearer
Bare of everything but particulars
Is a Bantu
The language of a people in southern Africa

He seeks to proceed from here to there
Please pass him on
Subject to these particulars
He lives
Subject to the provisions
Of the Urban Natives Act of 1925
Amended often
To update it to his sophistication
Subject to the provisions of the said Act
He may roam freely within a prescribed area
Free only from the anxiety of conscription
In terms of the Abolition of Passes Act
A latter-day amendment
In keeping with moon-age naming
Bearer's designation is Reference number 417181
And (he) acquires a niche in the said area
As a temporary sojourner
To which he must betake himself
At all times
When his services are dispensed with for the day
As a permanent measure of law and order
Please note
The remains of R/N 417181
Will be laid to rest in peace
On a plot
Set aside for Methodist Xhosas
A measure also adopted
At the express request of the Bantu
In anticipation of any faction fight
Before the Day of Judgement. (1975)

Sipho Sepamla (S. Africa)

The sounds begin again

The sounds begin again;
the siren in the night
the thunder at the door
the shriek of nerves in pain.

67

Then the keening crescendo
of faces split by pain,
the wordless, endless wail
only the unfree know.

Importunate as rain
the wraiths exhale their woe
over the sirens, knuckles, boots;
my sounds begin again.

Dennis Brutus (S. Africa)

Night knife

At the flick
of a knife
night plunges
sharply on the tender
flank of Soweto

Morning shrieks
like sirens
bloodwet with dew

And the day
sprawls empty
gaping in deathly surprise
like a slit throat.

Barolong Seboni (Botswana)

Further questions on this section may be found on page 101.

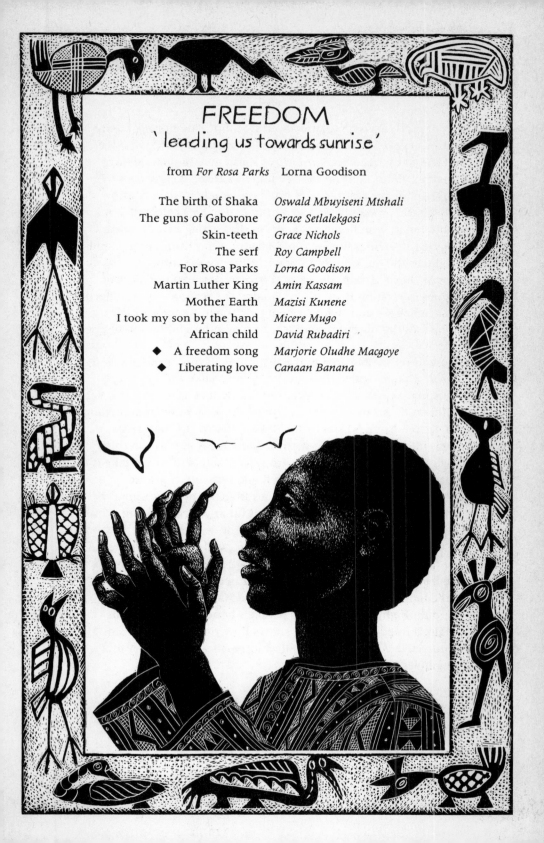

FREEDOM
'leading us towards sunrise'

from *For Rosa Parks*   Lorna Goodison

Before reading

The poems in this section are about freedom. The first six poems
describe action for freedom and the last group explore what we
understand by freedom. *The birth of Shaka* and *The guns of Gaborone*
remind us about fighting for freedom in Africa. *Skin-teeth* and *The
serf* are about the resistance of ordinary people to slavery and
oppression; *For Rosa Parks* and *Martin Luther King* celebrate a man
and a woman who became leaders in that struggle in America.
Mother Earth echoes the ideas of Martin Luther King's dream and
introduces the question of how we influence the future. *I took my
son by the hand, African child* and *A freedom song* explore ideas of
freedom in relation to children. Finally, the section – and, indeed,
the anthology – ends with a poem by Canaan Banana which
emphasises the importance of freedom as a foundation for all else
in life.

1 Do you remember that at the beginning of this anthology you
  wrote a poem called 'Love is . . .'? Poems like this are very
  personal expressions of what something means to you. It is very
  difficult to define freedom, without thinking of what you want
  to be free from. So start off by taking the words 'FREE FROM . . .'
  and finishing the phrase with as many ideas as you can think of,
  e.g. 'Free from prison', 'Free from pain', etc. You could take it in
  turns to go round the class and if you write each phrase on a
  separate piece of paper you can arrange the phrases into a
  rhythmic chanting poem and put it up in your classroom. You
  could do the same thing with the words 'FREE TO . . .'

2 If you look at your freedom chart, you will see that in order to
  be free from some things you need other things. For example, to
  be free from hunger and illness, you need nutritious food.
  Freedom charters, such as the United Nations Declaration of
  Human Rights, are based on people's basic needs and rights.
  Make a freedom wheel that shows how rights and freedoms are
  connected. Add as many rights and needs as you can. A few
  examples have been given.

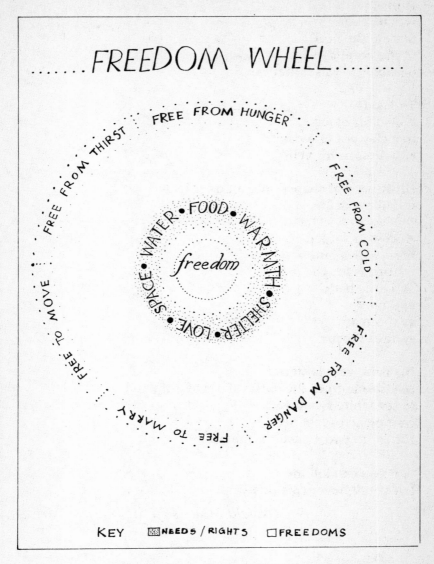

FREEDOM WHEEL

FREE FROM HUNGER
FREE FROM THIRST
FREE FROM COLD
FREE TO MOVE
FREE FROM DANGER
FREE TO MARRY

WATER · FOOD · WARMTH · SHELTER · LOVE · SPACE

freedom

KEY ▨ NEEDS / RIGHTS ☐ FREEDOMS

3 What does 'being free' mean to you? Have a class discussion (or a debate) about this statement: 'There cannot be total freedom in society: one person's freedom will inevitably limit someone else's.'

71

The birth of Shaka

His baby cry
was of a cub
tearing the neck
of the lioness
because he was fatherless.

The gods
boiled his blood
in a clay pot of passion
to course in his veins.

His heart was shaped into an ox shield
to foil every foe.

Ancestors forged
his muscles into
thongs as tough
as wattle bark
and nerves
as sharp as
syringa thorns.

His eyes were lanterns
that shone from the dark valleys of Zululand
to see white swallows
coming across the sea.
His cry to two assassin brothers:

'Lo! you can kill me
but you'll never rule this land!'

Oswald Mbuyiseni Mtshali (S. Africa)

The guns of Gaborone
(*Ditlhobolo Tsa Gaborone*)

June
Seetebosigo
    the month of shivering
    by the fireside
We were clustered like winter chickens
    dried saliva had trickled to our ears
    and our knees were pressed to our chins
The enemy fell on us
    like locusts at sunset

Gaborone
Shook with amazed suprise
Man and home crumbled into nothingness
Ten and more died for no provocation
June,
wrapt us with a riddled blanket

You,
Unfortunate,
You are cursed,
Terrorist
Butcher
Who refuses to acknowledge life
has set like the sun
Do you know that I have
stronger-armed brothers, my defenders, your age mates
who will ask you questions with the whisk of a whip?

I was there
You were blind
I listened
You were dumb
The country was bathed in blood
Gatwe
It is said
that

'Ntwa Kgolo ke ya molomo'
The battle is informed
by integrity
But you lacked ears
Tell me —
Does your book have the story of David and Goliath?

You who died
sleep in peace
Bana ba thari e ntsho
a luta continua
Lo e lole
You have fought

Grace Setlalekgosi (Botswana)

Translated from Setswana

Skin-teeth

Not every skin-teeth
is a smile 'Massa'

if you see me smiling
when you pass

if you seem me bending
when you ask

Know that I smile
know that I bend
only the better
to rise and strike
again

Grace Nichols (Guyana)

The serf

His naked skin clothed in the torrid mist
That puffs in smoke around the patient hooves,
The ploughman drives, a slow somnambulist,
And through the green his crimson furrow grooves.
His heart, more deeply than he wounds the plain,
Long by the rasping share of insult torn,
Red clod, to which the war-cry once was rain
And tribal spears the fatal sheaves of corn,
Lies fallow now. But as the turf divides
I see in the slow progress of his strides
Over the toppled clouds and falling flowers,
The timeless, surly patience of the serf
That moves the nearest to the naked earth
And ploughs down palaces, and thrones, and towers.

Roy Campbell (S. Africa)

For Rosa Parks

And how was this soft-voiced woman to know
that this 'No'
in answer to the command to rise
would signal the beginning
of the time of walking?
Soft the word
like the closing of some aweful book
a too-long story
with no pauses for reason
but yes, an ending
and the signal to being the walking.
But the people had walked before
in yoked formations down to Calabar
into the belly of close-ribbed whales
sealed for seasons
and unloaded to walk again
alongside cane stalks tall as men.

No, walking was not new to them.
Saw a woman tie rags to her feet
running red, burnishing the pavements,
a man with no forty acres
just a mule
riding towards Jerusalem
And the children small somnambulists
moving in the before day morning
And the woman who never raised her voice
never lowered her eyes
just kept walking
leading us towards sunrise.

Lorna Goodison (Jamaica)

Martin Luther King

Under Abraham's vacant eyes
He proclaimed a dream
A dream
That blossomed a sun
Where darkness had reigned
A dream
That bestrode the eagle
With ringing heart
Wheeling high above
Flailing truncheons thudding
On bare flesh
From rocky desert
He carved a valley
Where soil and clouds
Embraced and fused
With the voice of man
Buried in his neck

Amin Kassam (Kenya)

Mother Earth
or the folly of national boundaries

Why should those at the end of the earth
Not drink from the same calabash
And build their homes in the valley of the earth
And together grow with our children?

Mazisi Kunene (S. Africa)

I took my son by the hand

I took my son
by the hand
felt the warm flow
of young blood
comfort my cold
heart

This way we trekked
five long miles
to attend celebrations

It was
the season of peace
Away with agitators
Love and brotherhood *juu*
Division and hatred *chini*!

We heard of
    selfless sacrifice
Condemned
    selfishness
Damned
    laziness
Extolled
    industry

Celebrated
     freedom
Carried bursting fruit baskets
high high high
on elevated haughty heads

Towards sunset
we set out
for home
my son's little warm hand
inside mine
he in his world
me in mine

Mother, he asked

Do we have
matunda ya uhuru
in our hut?

I laughed foolishly

Mother!
Yes son
Do we have
some?

Silence

May I eat one
when we get there?
Move on son
darkness is looming fast
around us.

Micere Mugo (Kenya)

African child

Why African child
Stand you dazed
Your eye gazing
Far far into
the distant haze
and ask
questions too silent
for answers –

African child
Your wings will grow
Then
You must fly.

David Rubadiri (Malawi)

◆   A freedom song

Atieno washes dishes,
Atieno plucks the chicken,
Atieno gets up early,
beds her sacks down in the kitchen,
　　Atieno eight years old
　　Atieno yo.

Since she is my sister's child
Atieno needs no pay
While she works my wife can sit
Sewing every sunny day,
　　With her earnings I support
　　Atieno yo.

Atieno's sly and jealous
Bad example to the kids
Since she minds them, like a schoolgirl
Wants their dresses, shoes and beads.

Atieno ten years old,
Atieno yo.

Now my wife has gone to study
Atieno is less free,
Don't I feed her, school my own ones,
Pay the party, union fee
    All for progress? Aren't you grateful,
    Atieno yo?

Visitors need much attention,
Specially when I work nights.
That girl stays too long at market
Who will teach her what is right?
    Atieno rising fourteen,
    Atieno yo.

Atieno's had a baby
So we know that she is bad
Fifty-fifty it may live
To repeat the life she had,
ending in post partum bleeding
    Atieno yo.

Atieno's soon replaced
Meat and sugar more than all
She ate in such a narrow life
Were lavished on her funeral
Atieno's gone to glory
    Atieno yo.

Marjorie Oludhe Macgoye (Kenya)

◆ Liberating love

Though I preach the sacred value of human life,
if I sit on my hands and watch the oppression of my people,
I am a hypocrite.

Though I approve of the goals of human liberation
and profess love for freedom,
if I do not act on this love it is worthless.

Though I think I can tell which way the wind is blowing,
if I let the moment to act pass me by,
I betray the imperative to love.

The people have suffered long; charity serves barely
to keep them alive. But charity by itself defuses
the will of the people to act.

Love is not defined from a book or a tradition —
it does not rest in its own abstract goodness;
it is shaped by the concrete needs of the people.

True love abhors evil; it rejoices in the struggle for the good.
On the path to triumph love can bear all things, hope all things
it will not surrender.

Our need for justice and human dignity is as dear as life itself:
if there are political slogans they shall fade away;
if there are exploitative economic systems
they shall crumble and be changed.

For mankind cannot live by slogans alone.

Man's right to freedom and dignity is a gift from God,
thus when people together demand liberation,
that which oppresses shall give way.

For before I knew what it meant to have dignity,
I would neither see clearly nor love freely.
But when I began to struggle
I discovered the true meaning of Love.

When we were slaves, we spoke as slaves,
   we understood as slaves,
we thought as slaves;
but as we became free,
we cast off the chains of servitude.
So Faith, Love and Hope must abide: these three;
but without freedom and dignity
they remain hollow shadows.

Canaan Banana (Zimbabwe)

Further questions on this section may be found on page 106.

QUESTIONS

LOVE

After reading

1   We have started with *Lullaby* (p. 3) because it reminds us that poetry is made to be read aloud. It looks like a very simple poem, but it has been carefully crafted by the poet to seem that way. Read the poem aloud. How do you think it should be read? Why do you think the poem repeats the same phrases?

2   Often poems that are easy to understand at first reading also have deeper levels of meaning when you read them again. *The Zulu girl* and *My will* (pp. 3 and 4) are about the things a loving mother passes on to her child. These, too, are not things that money can buy.

> **a**   Make a list of the things that these two mothers want to give their children. Which of these would you most like to inherit?
>
> **b**   What things do you think it is important that parents pass on to their children?

3   *The beloved* and *And when you balance on your head* (pp. 5 and 6) are praise-songs to beautiful women. Both poets compare the women to other things.

> **a**   What sort of things are the women being compared with?
>
> **b**   Why do you think the poets have chosen these images?

Notice that the comparisons are sometimes direct, as in Okot p'Bitek's poem where he says, 'Your long neck/Resembles the alwiri spear.' These direct comparisons of one image with another (neck/spear) are called **similes** and they are intended to convey the strength of the poet's ideas and feelings. If you look at these two poems you will see that, by comparing the women directly with other natural objects, the poets strengthen the feeling you get of their beauty and grace. Sometimes, however, the comparisons are implied, such as: 'And the wild white lilies/Are shouting silently/To the bees and butterflies!' We know that the lilies are not really shouting to the bees and butterflies but when the poet says that, he is suggesting that all the natural world appreciates the woman's beauty. At the same time he is involving our senses of sight, smell and hearing by creating these images. This sort of comparison, when two things are compared without any direct link word such as 'like', 'as' or 'resembles' is called a **metaphor**.

    c Can you find the similes and metaphors in these poems? Which do you think are most effective?

4 The last three poems in this section are about changes in love.

    a If you could write the meaning of Shakespeare's poem, *Let me not to the marriage of true minds*, (p. 7) in one sentence, what would you write?

    b Do the poems *Armanda* and *The mulatta as Penelope* (pp. 7 and 10) prove him right or wrong? Have the feelings of the lovers in these poems changed?

    c In *The mulatta as Penelope* why does the poet say that her son will hear 'a different heartbeat'? Why is this a love poem?

5 Look at the way *The mulatta as Penelope* is written.

    a How many images connected with the sea can you find? A series of connected images like this is called a **sustained metaphor**.

    b What do you think this adds to the effect of the poem?

6 Write a love poem yourself. It could be a poem to one or both of your parents or a poem to someone real or imagined whom you love. Note down the images that come to your mind when you think about that person. Will your poem be written about something the person you love has done, or will it be about what you think love is? Or will it be a sort of descriptive list using lots of similes and metaphors, like some of those that you have read? If you are musical, you could make this into a love song.

7 You could write your poem as a special sort of list poem where each line begins 'LOVE IS . . .' and you finish the line. For example, you might say,

    '*Love is* the hungry mother giving her child bread' or
    '*Love is* the lioness fierce for her cubs'.

This sort of poem can be made as a whole class with each person contributing a line.

A closer look

Let me not to the marriage of true minds
                                 William Shakespeare (p. 7)

This poem is a **sonnet**. A sonnet is a poem written in 14 lines of iambic pentameter (explained below) and which concentrates on a single subject. In this sonnet Shakespeare compares love to various things that do not change at all, eg a star used by sailors to guide a course of a ship (bark).

1   What are 'impediments'? What do you think 'the marriage of true minds' is? Discuss what the first two lines mean.

2   Why is the height of the star measured? What does the poet mean when he says that you can measure the height of the star but not its worth? How can you apply this to love?

3   **a** The poet says that Time has a sickle. What do you do with a sickle? What does Time do with his sickle?

   b In Shakespeare's day the word 'fool' could mean a servant. Why is Love 'not Time's fool'?

When poets suggest that abstract things (like Time and Love) can do or feel or be what a human being could do or feel or be (like using a sickle) this is called **personification** (making a thing like a person).

4   **a** What do the last two lines mean? Can you write them as a plain English sentence?

   b Is there a double meaning in the words 'nor no man ever lov'd'? What might the poet be suggesting?

When the meaning of something is not clear and there could be two ways of understanding what is said, it is said to be **ambiguous**.

5   Shakespeare was famous for his use of a rhythm (also called a **meter**) called **iambic pentameter**, which is a name based on Greek words. The pentameter bit tells you that there are five strong beats to each line and the iambic part tells you where strong beats and light beats come. Every syllable of a line has a beat. In iambic pentameter, the strong and light beats alternate, with the light beat always coming first. Try saying the first two lines aloud and listening to the strong beats. It will sound like this (I have marked the strong beats ^{1} and the light beats x):

$$x \quad ^1 \quad x \quad ^1 \quad x \quad ^1 \quad x \quad ^1 \quad x \quad ^1$$
Let me not to the marr/iage of true minds

$$x \quad ^1 \quad x \quad ^1 \quad x \quad ^1 \quad x \quad ^1 \quad x \quad ^1$$
Ad/mit im/ped/i/ments. Love is not love

There are lots of other meters, but iambic pentameter is the most common regular rhythm for poetry in English and it is useful to know the technical term, as a quick way of describing this rhythm.

6   One of the special things about a sonnet is the way that it rhymes. You can find out the pattern of the rhymes (or **rhyme scheme**) for yourself, by putting letters at the end of the lines to show which words rhyme with which. You use the same letter for the same rhymes, so you would put A next to 'minds' and again next to 'finds', B next to 'love' and again next to 'remove', C next to 'mark' etc. Sometimes the rhymes are not very close, such as 'doom' and 'come', but they are close enough. What rhyme scheme would this sonnet have? The pattern should look like this: ABABCDCDEFEFGG.

7   Another interesting thing about a sonnet is that although it is always about one subject, there is usually a break in it where the poet looks at the subject from a slightly different angle. Where do you think the break is here? How has the poet's way of looking at the subject changed?

8   As you go through this anthology, look out for other sonnets and see how the basic sonnet pattern is changed. You might like to try writing a sonnet yourself: once you get the rhythm right, it isn't as difficult as it seems.

IDENTITY

After reading

1   All these poems are written as if someone is talking directly to the reader. None of them rhyme. Look particularly at *What is man?* and *Africa* (pp. 14 and 17). There are two voices within both these poems. What stops the poems from just being conversations? Is it something to do with the rhythms of the lines or the words the poet chooses and where she or he puts them? Look back at the poems and discuss what you think makes them poems and not prose.

2   *Holding my beads* (p. 14) is a very short but strong poem about womanhood. There are many poems and songs about what it is to be a woman or a man. In small groups, discuss what being a woman/girl or a man/boy means to you. Then, if you can, write a poem or a piece of prose about it.

3 Many of these poems look ahead to the future. Choose two and compare the poets' ideas about their identity and the future. For example, the last line of *Protest from a Bushman* is pessimistic: 'I live in sick apprehension,' but the end of *I, too, sing America* focuses on a positive future when: 'They'll see how beautiful I am/And be ashamed'.

These two poets see their futures very differently. You could try and explain why their feelings are different, or choose two other poems and discuss how the poets see their future.

4 In *Piano and drums* and *Once upon a time* (pp. 18 and 19), Gabriel Okara explores how the African's sense of his or her own identity is affected by the influence of European culture, but from two different points of view. The father in *Once upon a time* regrets the compromises he has made and the loss of his dignity and pride, and wants 'to unlearn all these muting things' the Europeans have introduced. For the poet in *Piano and drums* the conflict within himself between his African heritage and the 'new horizons' of Europe is symbolised in the 'jungle drums and the concerto'. Neither poem offers an answer to the conflict. In a small group discuss and compare the issues of identity in the poems.

5 Many of these poems are about identify emerging from conflict: for example, in *Africa* (p. 17), David Diop refers to 'black blood spilt over the fields'; in *We New World Blacks* (p. 23) Grace Nichols talks of the pull of the naval string 'in spite of ourselves', and in *The graceful giraffe cannot become a monkey* (p. 15) Okot p'Bitek writes of the struggle between the old traditions and modern ways. Write a story about someone (it could be you) becoming sure of their identity (who they are, what they believe in and what they want to do with their lives) through some sort of struggle or conflict.

6 The poem, *I speak for the bush* (p. 20) is about the differences between town and country life. Write a short play about a country person who comes to the city for the day. Use the ideas in the poem, anything else you have read and your own experience to help you write your play. You may do this on your own or in a small group. When you are satisfied with your play, try acting it out in front of the rest of the class.

7 Read *I, too, sing America* and *We New World Blacks* again (p. 23). In small groups, discuss how the poets relate their experiences as black people in America and the Caribbean to their African roots.

8 Write a poem about identity. If you want to write about yourself, you could start by looking at the web you drew of all the things you think are important about your own identity. Think how you could describe yourself in an original way: are there any images that you think describe you well? You can write your poem as a praise-song if you wish. If you would find it easier, write a poem about a group identity: your family or your nation, for example.

A closer look

The graceful giraffe cannot become a monkey
Okot p'Bitek (p. 15)

This extract comes from a long poem called *Song of Lawino* about the conflict between old and new ways.

1 Who is Lawino talking to in the poem?
2 What has Lawino's husband based his ideas of beauty on?
3 **a** How does Lawino react to her husband's complaint? How does she turn her husband's complaint into a praise-song for herself and her people?
   b What impression do you get of Lawino's character? How has that impression been created?
4 Some poems have lines in regular groups of the same length (eg groups of four lines together) throughout the poem. A regular group of lines is called a **stanza**. When the lines of a poem are not in regular groups of the same length (like here), each group is called a **verse paragraph**. Look at the verse paragraph that begins 'Listen,/my father comes from Payira . . .'
   a How does Lawino see her identity?
   b Who is surer of her/his identity: Lawino or her husband? Why do you say so?
5 What does the title of the poem, *The graceful giraffe cannot become a monkey*, mean? Look at the images in the verse paragraph that begins 'Listen,/Ostrich plumes differ . . .' Why has the poet chosen these images?
6 **a** Why do you think the poet has included the passage about ringworm? What has this got to do with identity?
   b Have you ever studied the meaning of different hairstyles and why people wear their hair in different styles? Write a poem about hair.

7   Compare this poem with *I speak for the bush* (p. 20). How are they similar or different?

Africa   *David Diop* (p. 17)

David Diop was born in France in 1927. His father was from Senegal and his mother from Cameroon, and he grew up in France and West Africa, aware of both cultures and traditions. He was deeply concerned about the question of independence from colonial rule.

1   Read the poem again. How does the information about Diop's background increase your understanding of the poem? Think about the question again after you have answered the other questions.

2   **a** Why does Diop say that black blood flows in his veins?

   b What does the poet see as the important factors in Africa's past history?

   c How does he feel these have shaped Africa's present?

3   The 'voice' that answers Diop sums up Africa's identity. It describes Africa as a tree.

   a What does the symbol of 'that tree young and strong' suggest?

   b What do you think 'the white and faded flowers' are?

   c Why do the fruits acquire 'the bitter taste of liberty'? Why does liberty taste bitter?

Do you think that a tree is a good symbol of Africa? Why?

4   Look at the lines from 'But your blood flows in my veins . . .' down to 'the slavery of your children'. What is the effect of the repetition? What does it make this part of the poem sound like? Have you ever heard a litany being chanted in a Catholic church? Do you think this might have anything to do with the poem?

DEATH AND THE ANCESTORS

After reading

1 **a** What contrasting images of death are there in Eric S.
   Ng'Maryo's poem (p. 27)? Are they similes or metaphors?
   (Look back at pp. 83 and 84 if you have forgotten what a
   simile or a metaphor is.)

   b Make some notes of the similes and metaphors that the poets
   use to describe death in the other poems in this section.

   c Compare your own ideas about death. You could look back at
   any notes you made before you read the poems. Write your
   own poem with the title 'What is death like?'

2 It is often said that in life there is death, and in death there is
life. Many of these poems tie life and death closely together. In
groups compare *What is death like?*, *Death*, *Death, be not proud* and
Death the leveller (pp. 27 and 31). Are the poets' ideas about the
relationship between life and death all the same?

3 Both *From the outside* and *To a small boy who died at Diepkloof
Reformatory* (p. 28) are poems about the deaths of people who broke
the law. In both poems there is a story suggested but not told: it is
as if we are there only at the end of the story. Imagine that you are
a reporter for a local paper and write the story of Madaza or of a
small boy in the Diepkloof Reformatory. Make it a story that will
catch the attention of your readers and affect their feelings. You
will need to decide on a headline for your story and if you write it
in columns it will look like a real newspaper.

4 *Death* and *From the outside* (pp. 27 and 28) describe funerals
rather as if they are the dead person's final performance on the
stage of life. Can you tell from each of the poems how the dead
person felt about life?

5 Work in groups of two or three. Tell a story about someone, as
if you were one of the mourners at his or her funeral: if you are
telling the story in public it will probably be complimentary, but if
you are telling the story privately to a group of friends it may not
be quite the same. Decide which way you will tell it. When you are
satisfied with your stories, present them to the rest of the class.

6 *Lament for the dead mother* (p. 31) is a poem about a child's love for and loss of her or his mother. Remember the poem called *Lullaby* (p. 3) about a mother's love for her child? Both are traditional poems. Compare them and try to explain how great emotion is conveyed through apparently simple poems.

7 The English poets, John Donne and James Shirley, wrote *Death, be not proud* and *Death the leveller* (p. 31) at roughly the same time in the early 1600s. Both poets are exploring the Christian view of the power of death. John Donne is saying that death is not final or terrible and that in the resurrection to eternal life 'death shall be no more'. James Shirley focuses on the vanity of people who think that their power on earth will protect them from death. What ideas do the two poems share about the causes of death and those affected by it? Which poem did you prefer?

8 In *Death the leveller* the poet uses objects to represent people. The technique of using symbols like this is called **metonomy**. The sceptre and crown represent kings, because kings carry these as symbols of their power; the scythe and the spade represent peasants, because peasants use these to work on the land. Notice how well the lines balance each other. What other poetic techniques can you find? (Look back at your notes on page 90).

9 Do you know any proverbs or stories that repeat the central ideas of the poems in this section? Try to collect a list.

10 *Prayer to the moon* and *The Ancestors* (pp. 32 and 33) take us back to the idea of the cycle of death and rebirths in the natural world as the moon waxes and wanes and in the spiritual world as the living relate to those who are already dead, the ancestors. In what ways is the cycle of life, death and rebirth part of your own life and beliefs?

11 Read *The Ancestors* aloud. You will probably notice the repetition of words and phrases. Make a note of them.

   a Does the poem sound like a prayer or a chant? What makes it sound like that? Is it a loud poem or a quiet poem?

   b Which sounds did you hear most often? Did they remind you of a whisper or the wind? Did this repetition help the sound and meaning of the poem?

The technique of using words to sound like their meaning (like 'whisper', 'rumble' or 'crash') is called **onomatopoeia**; it adds to the sound effect of the poem and can emphasise the meaning.

   c Can you think of any other words that are onomatopoeiac?

The poet made the poem sound like the wind or spirits passing, by using lots of words with long vowel sounds (like 'are') and with 'w', 's' or 'sh' sounds. The technique of starting words or syllables that are near each other with the same consonant sound is called **alliteration**. It is a way of drawing attention to the words, linking them together and making the poem more pleasing to hear. In some literary traditions it has been used as an alternative to rhyme. Look at these lines: 'The passing wind/the spirit that whirls the leaf/knows it perhaps.'

You will notice that the poet has alliterated the 'p', 's' and 'w' sounds. He has also repeated the 'i' sound (as in 'spirit'). Repeating vowel sounds that are near each other is called **assonance**. So you could say that here the poet uses onomatopoeia, alliteration and assonance to make the lines sound more like the wind and to make the meaning of the poem come across more clearly.

A *closer look*

To a small boy who died at Diepkloof Reformatory
Alan Paton (p. 28)

For 13 years Alan Paton was principal of a boys' reformatory in Johannesbury and he has written poems and short stories about his experiences there. This poem is about the death of a small boy in his care. Paton makes the poem sound like an official statement at a funeral service. As he buries the child ('commits his body to the earth' as the words of the Christian burial service put it) he is deliberately pompous: there are many long words and long sentences.

When you have read the poem again, ask yourself why Paton does this: what point is he making about the authorities and the waste of a young life? The more Paton emphasises the bureaucracy that surrounded the small boy 'in care', the more lost the lonely child seems. The tone of the poem is **ironic**: Paton means the opposite of what he says. Although he seems to be supporting authority, he is really questioning the values of a society that fails the young and helpless.

1   If you can, find a copy of a Christian burial service and compare the words of the service with the words of the poem. This will help you to see how Paton has adapted it for his own purpose. For

example, compare the end of the service with Paton's ending to the poem. Who is 'the great Judge-President'?

2 a What clues are there in the first section to the poet's feelings for the dead child? In what way is the child an offender and in what way is he innocent?

b What other contrasts does the poet make in the first section?

3 a Which documents does Paton refer to in the poem? How do you think the following lines should be read? 'Clerks are moved to action by your dying;/Your documents, all neatly put together,/Are transferred from the living to the dead.' What is the poet suggesting here about the attitude of those in authority to the boy?

b How and why does the tone change in this section? What images does Paton introduce as a contrast to the officials and the clerks with the documents? Can you find out the boy's name ('meaning, in white man's tongue, he is arrived')?

4 a Why is the boy now: 'enfolded in the sole embrace/of kindness that earth ever gave to you'?

b Paton uses the image of the earth embracing the boy for the rest of this section: look for examples of this sustained metaphor. (See page 84 if you have forgotten what this is.)

5 a In the last section, Paton talks about the 'warrant of committal'. What is this? What offence do you think the boy had committed?

b Paton says that millions of men are 'in complicity' with this offence, which means that they allow it to happen. What comment do you think Paton is making on the structure of South African society?

c Paton uses the word 'commit' ambiguously when he says 'So do I commit you'. What does he mean?

6 a Look back through the poem: how does Paton create the impression of the youth and vulnerability of the boy who died? What is ironic about the last four lines of the poem? (See p. 29).

b What did the real Judge-President who sentenced the boy to the reformatory suggest as his reason for this? How do we know that Paton does not approve of the sentence or agree with the reason? How will the sentence of the 'great Judge-President' contrast with the sentence that the real Judge-President of the court gave the boy?

7   Having looked at the poem in greater depth, how would you now describe the tone of the poem? Why do you think Paton wrote the poem? Did you like it? Do you think that writing poems is an effective way of changing society?

8   Write a scene between Paton and a friend after the boy's burial in which Paton explains how he feels.

Christine   *Barbara Burford* (p. 30)

Christine is a poem that tells a story: a **narrative** poem. The story is of a woman who is expecting a baby but it is still-born. From the little that the poet tells us we can guess the rest of the story: the clues are in the tone of the poem and the words and phrases the poet has chosen.

Azaleas are small bushes that have very beautiful flowers of many colours. They bloom in the early Spring: in Europe and America this would be in April.

1   Who is Christine?

2   What was the woman's first reaction to knowing she was pregnant? How do you know?

3   How does the poet link the idea of the growing child and the woman's growing love? What images does she choose?

4   The poet introduces another 'voice' in the second section of the poem. Whose voice is it? Why does it say the woman is brave but perhaps she'll change her mind? What tone do you think this part should be read in?

5   How does the poet contrast life and death in the third section? What has happened? Pick out some of the words she chooses to capture the way the woman feels. What sort of words are they? How do they make you feel? What does the poet mean when she says the mother listened to 'love clang in a kidney-dish' and 'could not look'?

6   Why do the nuns say it is 'kind providence'?

7   **a**   Why doesn't the woman know where her daughter is buried? Do you think it is important to know where someone you love is buried?

    b   There are many hints in this poem that the woman does not get much support or sympathy from people around her and that she is not in control of her own life. Why do you think this is?

VILLAGE LIFE

After reading

1 In *Inside my Zulu hut* and *The magnificent bull* (pp. 36 and 37) we can hear the pride and love of the poets for features of village life.

    a All the things inside the hut are used in daily life; how does the poet give us the impression that he is very satisfied with his hut and his life?

    b How is the picture of power and beauty built up in the traditional Dinka poem?

    c Compare the similes you thought of before you read the poems: are any of your similes like the Dinka images?

    d Notice how the rhythm of the Dinka poem changes in the last six lines and words 'water', 'spear' and 'river' are repeated: why do you think this is? When do you think the Dinka people might say this poem?

2 *Zebu* (p. 37), like *The magnificent bull*, is a poem that relies on repetition and images. It sounds almost like a chant or like *The Song of Solomon* from the Old Testament of the Bible. Try to write a poem yourself in the style of one of these poems: if it is going to appeal to people and be remembered, it will have to have lots of strong images, and repeated patterns of rhythm and language.

3 Did you notice something about *Zebu* that made it slightly different from the first two poems? The poet has made his description more humorous. First he builds up exaggerated images of strength, beauty and power; find some of these. Then Ranaivo adds something which is more realistic but unexpected, and which makes the description sound funny rather than serious.

    a Where does he do this? What effect does this have? Does it spoil the poem?

This technique of moving quickly from the realistic to the ridiculous is called **bathos**. It is a technique often used in jokes. For example, 'Your eyes are like limpid pools — of stagnant water!' Do you know any jokes like this?

    b Read *The beard* again (p. 42). Has the poet used bathos here? Explain your answer and the effect on the poem.

4 *An African thunderstorm* and *Drought* (pp. 38 and 39) show how the poets have chosen words carefully to create the mood of the poem.

95

a Read *An African thunderstorm* again out loud: what impression
do you get of the storm? How has that impression been
created?

b What does Rubadiri compare the wind to?

c Make a list of all the words that are to do with movement or
sound. Notice that some of the words sound like their
meaning eg 'rumble, tremble and crack'. Can you remember
the name of the technique of using words that sound like
their meaning? (See page 91 if you have forgotten.)

Now read *Drought* again and list all the words to do with heat and
exhaustion. Make up a list for yourself of words that you could use
for a poem about rain, wind, fire, or the sun. Try to include
onomatopoeia and alliteration (see pp. 91 and 92). When you have
written your first draft of the poem, look through it again and see if
you could add anything or change any of the words to intensify the
mood of the poem and make it more vivid.

5 The group of poems that includes *Grass will grow, I am becoming
my mother, Old Granny, The sweet brew at Chitakale, Gossips, The beard,
The poor man* and *The lazy man* (pp. 39–43) are all about people in
the village, their thoughts, their appearance and their behaviour.
Which do you think is the truest to life? (There is no 'right answer'
to this question – you will have to discuss the poems in small
groups and try to show each other why you think the poets have
expressed the truth so effectively and really described people as
they are.)

6 Read *The poor man* and *The lazy man* again. What sort of people
are described? Both poems describe what the people do and at the
same time tell us about their characters. Write a poem like this
about someone, for example: 'The rich man' or 'The miserable
man', or write a poem of contrasts: 'The rich woman and her maid'
or 'The blacksmith and his wife' where the behaviour of the two
people reveals their characters and relationship.

7 *The sweet brew of Chitakale* and *The beard* are both poems about
the relationship between village people and people from outside
the village. In small groups discuss the two poems. What do you
think the poets are telling us about the villagers and the outsiders
and how they see each other?

8 Read *Grass will grow* again. This, like many of the poems, gives
us insights into the values and beliefs of the village people and their
ability to withstand hard knocks in life. As a class, discuss how the

poets present these values and qualities.

9 *The sweetest thing* (p. 44) is a riddle poem and we are half-way through the poem before we know what the sweetest thing is.

> **a** What did you think the sweetest thing would be?
> **b** What three things does the poet say that sleep is sweeter than? Why does he include salt?
> **c** What or who are the numerous millions who arrive to disturb the sleeper?

Write your own riddle poem using this one as a model, but don't say what the answer is until the end. Read your poem to the rest of the class and see if they can guess the riddle before you tell them.

10 Many of the poets here use repetition. They repeat rhythms, sentence patterns, words and sounds. In the introduction we asked you to find out how passing a poem on by word of mouth affects the way it is shaped. You will have found that poems that are part of the oral tradition use a lot of repetition.

> **a** Why is repetition so important in oral poetry?
> **b** What else have you noticed about the way that poems from the oral tradition are shaped? Think about the traditional songs and stories you know. Discuss your ideas as a class.

A closer look

Grass will grow   *Jonathan Kariara* (p. 39)

1 Who is speaking in the poem? Who is she or he speaking to? What does she or he pray to have and not to have?

2 What do we learn about the speaker's expectations in life? What do these lines tell us about his or her character? 'Lord send a little rain/For grass will grow'

3 When a line is repeated in a poem, so that you know when to expect it, it is called a **refrain** or **chorus** and often the audience join in to say it. (You can probably think of songs like this.) It is also a technique used in church services, to include the congregation in the prayers. How does Jonathan Kariara use the technique here, rather differently?

4 **a** Why does the speaker associate madness with the moon?

> **b** What frightens the speaker most about madness? What is the difference between all the other disasters that he is prepared

to accept with fortitude and '. . . moon hard madness/To lodge snug in my skull'?

5   Discuss the statements below. Which of them do you agree with?

- This is a poem about hardships.
- This is a poem about facing adversity with courage.
- This is a poem about fears.
- This is a prayer for an easy life.
- This is a poem about going mad.
- This is a poem about the moon.
- This is a poem about nature's ability to heal scars.

6   Compare this poem to *My will* (p. 3). How are they similar and how are they different? Write your own prayer poem about the things that you most want in life and most fear.

The sweet brew at Chitakale   *Jack Mapanje* (p. 41)

1   Where do you think the old woman is? What is *thobwa*?
2   What do you notice about the amibiguity of the word 'stirs' in the lines: 'She uncovers the basket lid from the jar and/Stirs attention with a gourdful of the brew'?
3   The poem is full of action and movement: notice how the different people in the second, third and fourth stanzas are described and compare them.
4   a How does Jack Mapanje increase the tension in the fourth stanza?
   b What would you say is the climax of the poem?
   c What actually happens? Why do you think the poet does not describe it?
5   What do you notice about the way the poem is structured? Look at the length of the stanzas, the rhythm of the lines and the way the poem begins and ends with the old woman.
6   What do you think the old woman and the passenger were each thinking? Try to explain their actions.

SEPARATION

After reading

1   When you read the last lines of *Letter from a contract worker*
(p. 47) how did you feel? Did they make you laugh or feel sad?
Why? Look back through the poem to see how Antonio Jacinto
built up our expectations so that the final statements were such a
let-down. You have already met this technique of building up the
importance or grandeur of something and then suddenly dropping
to a very ordinary level. (See p. 95.) How do these lines affect the
way we feel about the characters in the poem?

2   *Letter from a contract worker*, *Refugee blues*, *Life is tremulous*,
Thoughts after work and *Yet another song* (pp. 47, 49, 51, 53 and 54)
are about people who have been forced to leave their old homes
and who feel like 'outsiders' or exiles, who do not really belong in
the places they are now in. Read these poems again and, working
in pairs or threes, note down:
   a the things which the 'exiles' in the poems missed most
   b the things that made them feel like 'outsiders'.

3   Have you ever moved to a different place or country? Describe
how you felt when you left your old home and moved to your new
home. Were you happy to go away? What were your first
impressions? What did you miss most? What were the most
difficult things to get used to? Perhaps you could write this
description as a letter to someone who still lives in your old home.

4   All these poems (except perhaps *The train*) are written as if the
poet is talking to the reader directly. In small groups, try to decide
what makes them sound so personal.

5   Many of these poems use **symbolism**: that means that they use
an object to suggest an idea, rather than expressing the idea
directly. For example, *The train* is describing a real journey, but it is
also suggesting that life itself is like a journey we all take. In small
groups, discuss how symbolism is used in *Epilogue* and *Footpath*
(pp. 50 and 52)?

6   Compare *Life is tremulous* with *Protest from a Bushman* (pp. 51
and 22). How do the images of the Bushman differ?

7   Read the poems *Thoughts after work*, *The renegade* and *Yet another
song* (pp. 53 and 54) again.

a What sort of work do the characters in these poems do? How has it affected their life-styles and their happiness?

b Have a class discussion about the following statements. Which of them to you agree with?

- It is easy to combine an African and a European life-style.
- If you want to progress you must leave African ways of life behind.
- If you cut yourself off from your roots you don't know who you are.

8 **a** Describe why the people in each poem are away from their own homes. (Perhaps the class could divide into ten groups and each group take one poem.)

b Compare this list of reasons with the lists you made before you read the poems. Are there reasons you didn't think of?

c Does the reason that the poet is away from home make a difference to the way she or he writes the poem?

d Each group could write a paragraph on the reason the poet has left home and how that has made her or him feel.

A *closer look*

Epilogue   *Grace Nichols* (p. 50)

Epilogue was written by a Black woman from Guyana who now lives in England.

1 This is a very short poem but it expresses important ideas about separation and a new beginning. What do you think the poem means? Work in small groups and quickly make a list of questions that you could ask that would help you to find the meaning of the poem.

2 Swap lists of questions with another group. In your group, discuss the answers to the questions on their list. If you need more questions you might find those below useful:

a Who is the poet talking about? Who has she been separated from?

b Which ocean has she crossed? Does the poet mean this only literally or does 'crossing an ocean' mean something else as well? (In other words, is the poem just about things that actually happened in geography and history or does 'crossing

the ocean' symbolise other changes that happen to people?
(See p. 99.)
c Why has the poet 'lost my tongue'?
d What does she mean when she says a new one has grown
  from the root of the old?
e Why is the word 'sprung' especially important?
f In what ways is this a poem about links as well as separations?
  Who is being linked with whom?

3   This poem tells you something about the development of
languages. You probably know that languages are dynamic (always
changing) and that they 'borrow' words and even grammatical
patterns from each other. What do you know about the languages
of the Caribbean? Try to find out about them and about the
influence of West African languages such as Twi and Fanti on the
Caribbean Creoles. Do you know what other languages have
influenced your own first language?

4   You can see that *Epilogue* is like an onion: it has lots of different
layers of meaning. It is about people and time: you could say it is
about: Grace Nichols herself, who left Guyana for England; all the
Caribbean people who left their homes to come to England; all
those people who left their own countries to go to the Caribbean in
the last few hundred years, especially all those who were taken
from Africa in slavery; all Black people all over the world whose
roots can be traced back to Africa over the centuries; all people all
over the world, as scientists think human life originated in Africa,
thousands of years ago. Write a page or more about what the poem
means to you. Try to show as many different layers of meaning as
you can.

POWER

After reading

1   Although *The flywhisk* (p. 58) is a contemporary poem about Jomo
Kenyatta and Dr Banda, it refers to the traditional symbol of the
power of African leaders and rulers. If you look back to James
Shirley's poem, *Death the leveller* (p. 31) you will find symbols of the

power of European rulers. In *The flywhisk* and in *The Oba of Benin* (p. 58), which is a traditional praise-song to a great ruler, look for images which suggest how the greatness of the African leaders is measured and how they maintain their power.

2 *A warrior sings his praises* (p. 59) is a different sort of praise-song. In it the warrior delights in his own strength and skill through describing his victories.

    a Make two lists, one for the warrior's names for himself and one for his names for his spear.

    b Read the poem again aloud. How do the names affect the sound of the poem? What else affects the sound of it? (You may want to look back to page 92 to remind yourself about alliteration.)

Could you write a praise-song for yourself (or for a friend or relative) listing your achievements? What names would you give yourself? When you write your praise-song, use alliteration rather than rhyme to give the poem its musical sound.

3 In *A baby is a European* (p. 61) the poem suggests similarities between the way that Europeans behave and the way babies behave. Write a paragraph about each stanza, explaining these similarities and pointing out the ironies (see page 92) in the poem. Why do you think we included this poem in the section on power?

4   **a** The next three poems (pp. 62–63) are all written in the first person ('I') but they all take a different point of view. For each poem, discuss who you think the speaker of the poem is.

    b Naomi Mnthali's poem *I remember* tells a story of changes of power and of hopes being raised and disappointed. Although it was written about Malawian Independence, it could describe other parts of Africa. In small groups try to decide what the poem means and explain how you feel about it.

5 *Pedestrian, to passing Benz-man* and *Building the nation* (pp. 62 and 63) are both deeply ironic poems which compare and contrast the rich and the poor. In each there is the suggestion that the rich have become rich and powerful by exploiting the poor. Find the clues that suggest this in the poem and then write a story about the past relationships between the pedestrian and the 'Benz-man'. How do you think their lives became so different?

6 To understand the full irony of Timothy Wangusa's poem, *Psalm 23, Part II* (p. 64), you will need to reread the original version in the Bible, which is about the protection and rewards that the Lord offers those who believe in Him. Timothy Wangusa has kept the pattern and style of the verses, but he has changed the words to make a mockery of the idea that this is a prayer. To imitate a style and form while changing the meaning ironically is called **parody**.

a You can see how the parody works, if you draw two columns and put the important phrases of the 23rd Pslam in one column and the words Wangusa has used instead in the other column.

b What do you notice when you compare the two lists?

c What sort of person do you think the speaker of the poem is?

d What job do you think he has?

7 Read *The renegade* and *Thoughts after work* again (pp. 54 and 53). What do you think these poems have in common with the poems you have just read?

8 The central image of David Rubadiri's poem *Begging AID* (p. 65) suggests that elders have become like circus performers that do tricks for their food. Rubadiri extends this image with references to 'manes that age in zoos', a 'Ringmaster' and 'amusing the gate for tips'.

a What do you think he means?

b What is the other important image in the poem and how does he bring that in?

9 *Western civilisation* (p. 66) is also an ironic poem and easy to understand. It gets its effect from the use of words like 'civilisation', 'intimate landscape', 'welcomes' and 'gratefully' in places where we do not expect to find them. In small groups discuss why these words are unexpected and the effect they have.

10 The last three poems focus on South Africa: *To whom it may concern* (p. 66) on the 'pass laws'; *The sounds begin again* (p. 67) and *Night knife* (p. 68) on the abuse of power in Black townships. Although *The sounds begin again* (1960s) and *Night knife* (1987) were written many years apart, what do you notice about the language and images of the poems? If you were to write a poem about Soweto, what would you want to emphasise? Can you write your own Soweto poem?

11 Many of these poems have criticised the way that people have behaved. Work in groups to make a list of 'Ten rules for rulers'. Compare your list to the lists of others in the class and agree a class list of ten rules.

12 Look through the poems again and collect a list of as many images of power as you can find. They may be one word images ('sirens, knuckles, boots' from *The sounds begin again*) or extended images (such as the elders as circus performers in *Begging AID*). Discuss your lists in small groups. What do you notice about the images?

A *closer look*

Stanley meets Mutesa   *David Rubadiri* (p. 59)

H. M. Stanley was an Englishman who travelled into the African interior; the poem tells the story of Stanley's journey into what is now Uganda. Find out where Stanley started from, where Mutesa's kingdom was and where the Nile and Nyanza are before you start work on this poem.

1   Because this is a narrative poem (see p. 94), the poet has used some of the traditional techniques of the storyteller. Ask someone to read the poem again aloud and as you listen, try to identify some of the techniques that keep you interested and involved. Listen out for tone and style, repetition, and vivid details that bring the story to life and create suspense. Discuss your impressions as a class.

2   The conversational style and rhythm of the beginning of this poem is very like the opening of T. S. Eliot's poem *The journey of the Magi* which is about the journey of the three kings to find the Christ child: 'A cold coming we had of it,/Just the worst time of the year/For a journey, and such a long journey:/The ways deep and the weather sharp,/The very dead of winter'.

What should be ironic (see p. 92) about the comparison of the journey of the three kings and Stanley's journey? Look at the line 'they bound for a kingdom' and the description of Stanley as: 'Its Khaki leader in front/He the spirit that inspired/He the light of hope'.

3   Look closely at the first three verse paragraphs, to the line 'He the light of hope'.

    a How has David Rubadiri used the sound of words to emphasise the meaning?

    b Find some examples of alliteration and assonance (see p. 92), repetition and **'imperfect' rhyme** (words sounding similar but not rhyming perfectly e.g. drum/skin). Why do they matter to the sound and feel of the poem?

4   In the fourth verse paragraph the pace of the poem changes.

a What does the poet describe to suggest the different behaviour and feelings of the marchers?

b From whose point of view have the first four verse paragraphs been presented?

5 Compare and contrast the two men, Stanley and Mutesa. Work in groups of two or three. Draw two columns. Head one STANLEY and the other MUTESA. Think of what the poem tells you about their appearance, behaviour, attitudes and roles as leaders and make lists under the headings.

6 The last verse paragraph describes Mutesa welcoming Stanley into his kingdom, but Rubadiri means us to understand much more from it. He invites us to make connections across centuries and continents. He helps us to do this by making ordinary things symbolic (see p. 99) of much more important things. For example, opening the gate of reeds does not just mean the gate to Mutesa's kingdom: it also suggests Africans welcoming Europeans into the heart of Africa. Rubadiri also changes the verb tenses from the past tense to the present. In groups discuss the symbolism of the poem and how the change of verb tense affects the meaning.

8 You have already noticed that there is irony in the poem. Some of the irony in this poem is of a special sort that is often found in plays. It is called **dramatic irony** (or sometimes **tragic irony**). It occurs when a character says something that conveys a different or more serious meaning to the audience (or readers) because they know more than the characters. For example, they may know that something terrible is going to happen. What would you say are examples of dramatic irony in this poem?

To whom it may concern   *Sipho Sepamla* (p. 66)

1 What is Sipho Sepamla's poem about? Copy the poem out but use two colours. Write the lines that sound as if they are taken from an official document in one colour and the lines that are the poet's comments in another colour, starting like this:

Bearer	(official document)
Bare of everything but particulars	(poet's comments)
Is a Bantu	(official document)
The language of a people in southern	
Africa . . .	(poet's comments)

    a Try having two people read the poem aloud in parts.

    b What sort of poem is this? Compare it with *Pslam 23, Part II*
    (p. 64).

2 Try writing a poem yourself using this parody technique (see
page 103). You will have to use formal language with no similes or
metaphors and you must insert your own comments into the text
of the poem. You could use a newspaper article or a paragraph
from a text book as the basis of your poem. Is it very different from
any other poem you have written?

3 Sipho Sepamla often uses **puns** which means that he plays on
the sound and meaning of words. For example, the opening lines
play on the similar sound of the words 'bearer' and 'bare' to make a
comment on the fact that although he has his pass, he has nothing.
Can you find other examples in the poem of puns like this?

4 **a** Rewrite the lines from 'Bearer's designation . . .' to
     'dispensed with for the day', in ordinary English.

    b What is the difference in tone between your version and the
     poet's?

    c Does the tone affect the way we see the pass-bearer? Why
     does he not have a name?

5 This poem may remind you of the Alan Paton poem *To a small
boy who died at Diepkloof Reformatory* (p. 28). Like Paton, Sepamla
uses the language of officials to make ironic statements about their
policies. Reread Alan Paton's poem and discuss the similarities and
differences between the two poems.

FREEDOM

After reading

1 Did you notice that many of the images in *The birth of Shaka*
(p. 72) were based on the natural world? Look back at the poem
and see how many you can find. Then write a poem yourself about
an animal or bird enjoying its freedom.

2 *The birth of Shaka* may remind you of the praise-songs like *The
Oba of Benin* and *A warrior sings his praises* (pp. 58 and 59). They all

find new ways of describing personal strength. Try to work out the story from the poem. You could then do some research: try your history teacher or books on the history of Southern Africa. Share your findings with the rest of the class and see how the facts you have discovered affect your understanding and enjoyment of the poem.

3 *The guns of Gaborone* (p. 73) was written during the night of the bombing of Gaborone by the South African commandoes, killing sleeping adults and children and destroying homes. Why do you think the poet asks 'Does your book have the story of David and Goliath?'?

4 Grace Nichols' poem, *Skin-teeth* (p. 74), relates to the people from Africa who were taken as slaves to the Caribbean and the Americas, and to their resistance to slavery. 'Skin-teeth' means baring your teeth.

> **a** Do you think this poem should be read loudly or quietly? (Try it both ways.)
>
> **b** Did you feel a sense of menace and threat in it? How do you think Grace Nichols has achieved that?

5 *Skin-teeth* and *The serf* (pp. 74 and 75) are both about ordinary people who did hard physical work for little or no reward. They were not heroes, nor were they famous, but they resisted their oppression.

> **a** How and why did they do this?
>
> **b** How do the poets build up dramatic tension in the poems, so that the last lines of both poems reflect contrast and change?
>
> **c** In what way are the women and the men in these poems resisting their oppression? In groups of three or four, discuss whether you think this sort of resistance is as important as the resistance of Shaka and other fighters for freedom.

6 Rosa Parks like Martin Luther King was important in the struggle of Black Americans for freedom and equality. Either write or tell a story about one of them or about anyone you know who has contributed to the struggle for freedom anywhere in the world. (You do not have to write about a famous person, but you may if you want.)

7 Martin Luther King said, in a famous speech in 1963, that he had a dream that one day 'little black boys and black girls will be able to join hands with little white boys and white girls and walk together as sisters and brothers.' He ended the speech by saying:

'When we let freedom ring from every village and hamlet, from every state and city, we will be able to speed up that day when all of God's children, black men and white men, Jews and Gentiles, Protestants and Catholics, will be able to join hands and sing in the words of the old Negro spiritual, 'Free at last! Free at last! Thank God Almighty, we are free at last!'

  a What links can you see between this and Mazisi Kunene's poem *Mother Earth* (p. 77)?

  b Sometimes *Mother Earth* is given a longer title: *Mother Earth, or the folly of national boundaries*. What are 'national boundaries' and what do they have to do with freedom?

8 Discuss whether *I took my son by the hand* (p. 77) is a poem about:

A mother's relationship with her son

Having pride in your country

National unity

Sharing celebrations with friends and neighbours

The difference between political slogans and everyday reality

9 The child in *I took my son by the hand* asks his mother a naïve question about the reality of freedom for them. In *African child* (p. 79) the question is 'too silent for answers'. In small groups, discuss:

  a What questions do you think the child is thinking of?

  b Why are they 'too silent for answers'?

10 When you have read *Liberating love* (p. 81), discuss how its 'message' could be applied to other poems in this section, or in the section on power. What connections can you find?

11 In groups of four or five have a discussion on the use and value of prisons. You might want to think about these questions:

- Do you think it is right to send people to prison for all crimes?
- Are prisons built to protect society, or to punish or re-habilitate prisoners?
- What alternatives to prison could there be?
- Should children be sent to prison?

A closer look

A freedom song   *Marjorie Oludhe Macgoye* (p. 79)

A freedom song is a narrative poem (telling a story), but it is a special sort of narrative poem called a **ballad**. Ballads were originally sung, but the term is now used for any lively poem in short stanzas which tells a popular story. Ballads usually involve love, war, adventure or death and often have a moral point or message. Because ballads are part of the oral tradition, and depend on being remembered, they make use of rhyme, rhythm and repetition and they sometimes have repeated lines at the end of each stanza which are called the chorus or refrain (see p. 97) so that the listeners can join in.

1 a Work in small groups to discuss what you learn about the character of Atieno, her aunt and uncle from the poem.

  b How does Atieno change over the years? What do you think makes her change?

2 Why do you think the poem is called *A freedom song*? Whose freedom is it about?

3 In this anthology you have read many ironic poems. The irony in this poem is very bitter. Pick out three lines that you think are especially ironic and explain why.

4 Read the poem through again out loud, listening especially to the rhyme and rhythm.

  a What do you notice about the pattern of each stanza? Which lines rhyme?

  b Is the rhythm regular? How many beats to the line are there?

  c What do you notice about the way the poet uses the name 'Atieno' in the poem?

When you have found answers to these questions, discuss what you think the rhyme, rhythm and repetition add to the poem.

5 Imagine you are Atieno. Think about what her life was like: use the hints in the poem to help you. Then write three extracts from her diary showing how she felt and what happened to her.

Liberating love   *Canaan Banana* (p. 81)

Canaan Banana is not only a poet, he was also the first President of Zimbabwe. It is one of the characteristics of African literature that many of Africa's political leaders are also poets and writers. It is hardly surprising then, that so much of African poetry is political. *Liberating love* is interesting not only in the way that it combines poetry and politics but also in the way that it examines the

Christian tradition of love and suffering.

1   *Liberating love* is based on a passage from the Bible: *I Corinthians 13*. To appreciate how Canaan Banana has used the Biblical passage you will have to read it and compare the original verses with his poem. What similarities do you notice?

2   In his letter to the Corinthians, St Paul emphasised the importance of love. How does Canaan Banana redefine love to suit an African context? Make a list of the ways he says you can show love for other people.

3   In older versions of the Bible, love used to be called 'charity'.

   a   How does Canaan Banana play on the word 'charity' in the poem? Compare lines 10–12 with verse 4 of *I Corinthians 13* and lines 13–15 with verse 5 of *I Corinthians 13*. How has Canaan Banana changed what the Bible says to suit the situation of his people?

   b   What 'book or tradition' do you think he is referring to and what do you think he means by saying love is not defined by this?

4   How has the poet interpreted verses 6 and 7 in lines 16–18? Is his view closer to the original here?

5   *I Corinthians 13* ends by referring to 'faith, hope and love but the greatest of these is love'.

   a   Lines 19–23 of the poem echo verse 8 in style but Canaan Banana is expressing different views. What do you think he means in lines 19–23?

   b   What does the poet believe is 'the true meaning of Love' (lines 27–30).

6   Compare the last two stanzas (lines 27–34) with verse 11 of *I Corinthians 13* and comment on the changes the poet has made. What is the historical and political meaning in the lines?

7   Read the whole poem through again. Do you like the sound of the poem? When you hear it now, does it sound more like a poem, a prayer or a political speech or a combination of all of these?

8   If you had to live *your* life by any slogan, which would you choose to live by? Write your slogan and explain to the rest of the class why you chose it.

GLOSSARY

This glossary of the technical terms you might use to talk about poetry tells you where you will find each term explained in the text. Examples are drawn from the poems.

Acknowledgements

The publishers would like to thank the following for permission to reproduce their copyright material:

Ad Donker (Pty) Ltd for the poem 'Protest from a Bushman' by Albert Malikongwa from *Voices from Within* eds Achmat Dangor and Michael Chapman; Professor Canaan Banana for 'Liberating Love'; Cambridge University Press for the poems 'Lullaby' by Akan (Kwabena Nketia in *Black Orpheus*, 3), 'Lament for a dead mother' by Ewe (Geormbeeyi Adali Morkry, in *Black Orpheus*, 4), 'The Ancestors' a Hottentot poem (*Les Pygmes de la Grande Sylve Ouest Equatorial*, by D Trilles), 'A baby is a European' by Ewe (Kafu Hoh, in: *Voices of Ghana*), 'The magnificent bull', a Dinka poem, 'Death' by Kuba, 'The sweetest thing' by Soussou, 'The lazy man' a Yoruba poem (from *Yoruba Poetry*, by Bakare Gbadamosi and Ulli Beier), 'The poor man' a Swahili poem (from *Swahili Poetry*, by L Harries) 'The Oba of Benin' by Bini (John Bradbury, in *Nigeria Magazine*), 'Prayer to the moon' a Bushman poem, 'The beloved' a Fulani poem (Malam Hampate Ba, in *Présence Africaine*) from *African Poetry* ed Ulli Beier (1966); Francisco Campbell Custodio and Ad Donker (Pty) Ltd for 'The Zulu Girl' and 'The Serf' by Roy Campbell; Faber and Faber Ltd for 'Refugee Blues' from *Collected Poems* by W H Auden; Heinemann Educational Books Ltd for 'The Sounds Begin Again' by Dennis Brutus from *A Simple Lust*, 1973; 'Piano and Drums' and 'Once upon a time' by Gabriel Okara from *The Fisherman's Invocation*, 1978, 'The Sweet Brew at Chitakale' by Jack Mapanje from *Of Chameleons and Gods*, 1981; Heinemann Kenya Ltd for 'And when you balance on your head' and 'The graceful giraffe cannot become a monkey' by Okot p'Bitek from *Song of Lawino*, 1966; Karnak House Publishers for 'Skin-teeth', 'Holding my beads' and 'Epilogue' © Grace Nichols; Mazisi Kunene for 'Mother Earth'; Longman Group UK Ltd for 'Armanda' by Jared Angira from *The Heritage of African Poetry* ed Isidore Okpewho, 1985; Albert Malikongwa for 'Life is tremulous; Naomi Sophie Mnthali for 'I remember'; Mĩcere M. Gĩthae Mugo for 'I took my son by the hand' from *Daughter of My People, Sing!*; New Beacon Books Ltd for 'My will', 'The Mulatta as Penelope', 'I am becoming my mother', 'For Rosa Parks' by Lorna Goodison, 1986; Stella Ngatho for 'Footpath'; David Higham Associates Ltd for 'I, too, sing America' by Langston Hughes from *Selected Poems*, Vintage Books; Oxford University Press for 'A warrior sings his praises' by Erinesti Rwandekyezi, from *The Heroic Recitations of the Bahima of Ankole* by H F Morris, 1964, 'Inside my Zulu hut' and 'The Birth of Shaka' © Mbuyiseni Oswald Mtshali, from *Sounds of a Cowhide Drum* by Mbuyiseni Oswald Mtshali, 1971; Oxford University Press East and Central Africa for 'Psalm 23, Part II' by Timothy Wangusa, 'The Flywhisk' by John Ruganda, 'Grass will grow' by Jonathan Kariara, 'A freedom song' by Marjorie Oludhe Macgoye, 'Building the nation' by Henry Barlow, from *An Introduction to East African Poetry* eds Jonathan Kariara and Ellen Kitonga, 1976; Jonathan Paton for permission to publish his father's poem 'To a small boy who died at Diepkloof Reformatory'; Présence Africaine for 'Africa' and 'The Renegade' by David Diop, first published as 'Afrique' and 'Le Renegat' in *Coups de Pilon*, Paris, 1956; Marian Reiner for the extract from 'How to Eat a Poem' by Eve Merriam from *JAMBOREE Rhymes for all Times* by Eve Merriam. Copyright © 1962, 1964, 1966, 1973, 1984 by Eve Merriam. All rights reserved; Proscovia Rwakyaka for 'The beard'; David Rubadiri for 'African child', 'Thoughts after work', 'Yet another song', Begging AID', 'An African thunderstorm' and 'Stanley meets Mutesa'; Barolong Seboni for 'Night Knife' from *Tribute* magazine; Sipho Sepamla and Ad Donker (Pty) Ltd, for 'To whom it may concern' by Sipho Sepamla; Grace Setlalekgosi for 'Gossips' and 'Guns of Gaborone' translated from Setswana by Leloba Molemo and David Rubadiri; Sheba Feminist Publishers for 'Christine' by Barbara Burford; Everett Standa for 'I Speak for the Bush', from *Poems from East Africa* eds David Cook and David Rubadiri, 1971; Virago Press for 'We New World Blacks' copyright © Grace Nichols, 1985 from *Fat Black Woman's Poems*, Virago Press, 1984.

The publishers have made every effort to trace copyright holders, but in some cases without success. We shall be very glad to hear from anyone who has been inadvertently overlooked or incorrectly cited and make the necessary changes at the first opportunity.